Like many of us I have read loads of leadership books, some good and some not so good; however, I have never read anything that captures 'the art and the science' (as Ian describes it) as well as this book does. He breaks down the components in a reader-friendly and easily digestible style and does so in a way that either the New Leader can equip themselves with the Bible, or any of us more experienced, who want to refresh our thinking, can dip in and out of the bits we need to remind ourselves of the most. The book is littered with real-life anecdotes that bring it to life and contains some of the very best quotes you can use for life. This is an absolute must for every leader's desk, never to gather dust in the library!

David Sheepshanks CBE DL, Founding Chairman of St George's Park, FA National Football Centre & Vistage Chair

Ian knows more about leadership than anyone else I've known. He has spent many years honing and crafting his leadership map, working closely with a huge variety of different businesses, and absorbing the thoughts of almost every key speaker and expert on leadership. This book is an all-encompassing guide to what it takes to be a brilliant leader, and I can't recommend it highly enough.

Patrick O'Luanaigh, CEO, nDreams

Clear, concise and perceptive – a great guide to leadership in business.

Stephen Dunford, Chairman of multiple tech businesses

Ian has been my business coach through the years that have seen Breathe grow from a small start-up to a thriving scale-up. He is one of my most valued advisors and has helped me make many difficult decisions. His skill lies in asking challenging questions, and *The Leadership Map* will help leaders tease out what questions they need to ask of themselves and their businesses.

Jonathan Richards, CEO, Breathe

This map is just bursting with ideas, examples and steps to take on your leadership journey. Keep it close: it is packed with relevance and steeped in experience.

Peter Joshua, Founder, Thecosystems

The Leadership Map shares a journey through engaging insight of building business and culture. Using analytical and practical guides, designed to encourage action from managers and leaders, the book focuses on strategy, people and execution within an organization – critical for building great businesses. An excellent reminder of leadership fundamentals.

Carol Blackford-Mills, Founder and MD, MRS Digital

The Leadership Map simplifies the incredibly complex challenges facing leaders of growing businesses today. The logical, easy-to-follow structure gives you the tools you need to become a better leader. This book is a must read that you'll find yourself coming back to again and again.

Dominic Gaynor, CEO, TeamSport Karting

I was in the audience when Ian gave his TEDx Talk and subsequently attended one of his 'Leadership Map' workshops. I was therefore thrilled when I heard that that wisdom and content he eulogizes were being committed to a book. Reading the manuscript, I'm delighted that Ian has successfully crafted an essential leadership blueprint on all the requisite areas needed to successfully run a business. I started my own company 30 years ago and I would have loved to have had access to this then; however, even for a long-established firm there is so much value in this book, allowing the reader to reflect and challenge themselves and their organization. *The Leadership Map* is a 12-piece (chapter) jigsaw puzzle and you need to successfully assemble all the pieces to complete the very best version of you, the leader, and for your organization to excel as a result. I implore you to read this book, invest your time and energy to properly assemble the elements of the map and you will have given yourself the very best chance of success.

Rob May, MD, ramsac and international keynote speaker

This is the kind of book you need to break down what leadership is and get inspiration on how to apply it in your daily work as a leader.

Jan Hansen, Owner, SAV Systems

Leading a business is all about culture, where you unite people around a common purpose. During that process, you come to recognize that people want to be valued and trusted. *The Leadership Map* offers you the practical tools, techniques and processes that will enable you to make this happen and in doing so help you build a more profitable, successful and sustainable business. I know – I've done it.

Jim Kirkwood, CEO, TTC Group (UK) Ltd

Ian Windle has done something unique. He's written a truly practical book about leadership! There are plenty of practical books about management, but so few on leadership, and so this book strives to reach new territory by delving into the practical world of leadership. Stephen Covey says that management is about climbing the ladder, and leadership is about knowing which wall to put the ladder against. In this amazing book, Ian shows us how to find the wall, how to choose the ladder, where to put the ladder and who to take on that journey up the ladder.

David Batchelor, Founder and MD, Wills and Trusts

Ian Windle gets strategy and has guided and supported us to a clearly defined and compelling strategic identity. Highly recommended!

Hugh Welch, European Managing Director, Kyocera SGS

The mentorship of this author, over the last few years, has culminated for me in a company so engaged they set their own goals and share in the profits. The only addition I would add to this fabulous book, is that a business coach is essential, as it can be lonely at the top in the early days.

Paul Martin, CEO Kelly's Storage

I feel immensely privileged to have been guided by Ian on my road to becoming a more effective leader but not a day goes by when it wouldn't be useful to turn to him for advice, so I'm really pleased that he's taken the time to write his own leadership handbook! There's no doubt that leadership can be complicated and difficult but with this book by your side, I guarantee you'll be well-equipped to deal with the challenges, develop successful strategy and build resilient, focused, engaged and effective teams.

David Smith, CEO S M Contracts Limited

The Leadership Map provides a clear and well-conceived approach to leadership and combines many topics into one very useful tool. This book is a must-read for any business leader regardless of where they are in their career; starting out, transitioning through management, or seasoned business owner. It is a 'career book' – one you will come back to again and again, each time finding something new and a new perspective.

Ben Beaumont, Managing Director, 48.3 Scaffold Design

THE
LEADERSHIP
MAP

The gritty guide to strategy that
works and people who care

IAN WINDLE

First published in Great Britain by Practical Inspiration Publishing, 2021

ISBN   9781788602242   (print)
      9781788602235   (epub)
      9781788602228   (mobi)

Contents

List of figures and tables

Figures

Tables

Introduction

The most dangerous leadership myth is that leaders are born – that there is a genetic factor to leadership. That's nonsense; in fact, the opposite is true. Leaders are made rather than born.

– Warren Bennis

Great leaders develop minute by minute, day by day, year by year. Their days are filled with knotty problems, challenges, opportunities and risks. They won't get everything right all the time, there will be highs and lows, their people will rise to the occasion and sometimes fail to show up. Their resilience will be tested at every turn. Ultimately, they will be successful in this infinite journey – they may lose a battle, but their eyes are firmly fixed on the long game: a vivid vision of the future towards which they are working. They build businesses that will endure, based on cultures that allow people to bring their whole selves to work and make the most of who they are. If the challenge of leadership excites you, then this book is for you. If you believe you were born a leader or are fixed in your ways of doing things, then put the book down and carry on as you are. But if you believe – as I do and as Warren Bennis does – that leaders are made not born, then read on.

Leadership is complicated, there is a lot to learn and it is a never-ending journey. Most leaders aren't trained in leadership – they just pick it up from their boss, from books and magazines and from high-profile leaders in the press. This can be confusing. You might be reading about Steve Jobs and his leadership style with Apple (which changed hugely between his first tenure as CEO and his second one), or Karren Brady, Vice Chairman of West Ham United Football Club, or Nelson Mandela, the anti-apartheid revolutionary and then leader of South Africa, or Sheryl Sandberg of Facebook. All are successful leaders – and all are completely different!

One day you are a manager, then the next you're asked to be a leader and you are supposed to know what to do – at least that was the case when I became Managing Director of Celemi Ltd back in 1997. Before we move on, though, let me explain the key differences between leadership and management. Leadership is about working 'on' the business, deciding where you are going to go as a business and setting a stretching vision. It's about understanding what makes you different from the competition and then inspiring, challenging, growing and developing your people to perform at their absolute best, towards achieving the vision. Management, on the other hand, is about working 'in' the business. It's about planning, organizing and controlling, and making sure things get done. As we work our way up the organizational ladder, we need to learn more leadership skills while still spending most of our time managing, whereas once we get to the top of an organization, we need to spend most of our time leading and less time managing. When I became an MD, I'd been on lots of courses, read numerous books and had even completed an MBA, but I didn't really have much of a clue about how to lead when I started! The good news for all of us, as Warren Bennis[1] puts it, is that leaders are made, not born.

This book isn't about personality or approach; rather, it is a practical guide to what leaders need to do to be successful. This book is for you if you are a small start-up, or running a large, successful business. The framework is the same, although the complexity is quite different. As a pragmatist, I like to have tools and processes that are thoroughly researched, that will help me do things consistently well over time to help me achieve my goals. I have provided many tools on the topics I am covering in this book with guidelines on how to use them. I hope this book will inspire you to be a better leader and give you tools, tips and techniques to support you.

Leadership can never be more about the leader than the led. When it is, be careful. If you are a leader or you aspire to be one, then ask yourself why? Why do you want to be a leader? The wrong motives will stress you and your organization; they will lead to a dysfunctional leadership team, poorly led people, awful meetings and a lack of clarity and alignment in the business. Whereas choosing to be a leader for the right reasons will be quite the opposite. Leadership is not easy: it is tough. As John F. Kennedy said at the Rice Stadium in 1962, 'We choose to go to the moon in this decade and do other things not because they are easy, but because they are hard.' If you want to be a leader, or are already a leader, a measure of

---

[1] Warren Bennis was an American scholar, consultant, author and pioneer of leadership studies.

how well you are doing is how hard you are finding it. If you are finding leadership easy, then you are probably not doing the right things. Do leadership well and you will find it to be both the most challenging and the most rewarding thing you'll ever accomplish.

In 2001 I led a change programme in a large public sector organization in the United Kingdom for almost 100,000 staff. The object was to understand the organization's 'core purpose' and translate it into providing exceptional customer service. It was a wonderful programme to work on. Over a six-month period, we designed the programme, road tested it in several departments and then through a train-the-trainer programme, started to roll it out. It was all going well.

I'd been on lots of management courses and read numerous books and even done an MBA, but I didn't really have much of a clue about how to lead when I started!

One Monday morning, two months into the roll-out, I was attending a board meeting to report on progress. We were in an oak-clad room, sitting around a large 12-seater mahogany table. The old brown leather chairs creaked as the directors moved in them and there was a smell of wood polish and coffee from the filter machine on the corner table. The agenda moved to our change programme and the chairman of the board leaned forward with a worried expression on his brow: 'Ian, I think we have a problem.'

This was not what I was expecting, and I must admit that the worried brow now transferred to my own forehead. He continued: 'The programme is getting stuck with middle management; our leaders simply aren't leading.' There was silence in the room. It seemed to last an eternity. 'What do they understand by leadership?' I responded. 'Good question,' he said. 'I don't know. Please go and find out.'

That interaction around the board table changed everything for me – it was a seminal moment in my business life. With another senior colleague, we interviewed about 30 middle and senior managers across all parts of the organization. We booked in an hour each of their time and had a set number of questions to help us understand what they thought leadership was and how they felt they were judged as leaders. Now for the scary part: we heard 30 different answers. They pulled documents out of drawers, proceeded to describe various leadership frameworks, told us what their job description was or just looked blankly back at us. It was very revealing and, as I found out, not entirely unusual in business. Most of all, it was worrying. These well-paid middle and senior managers, most with large groups of employees working for them, had no consistent understanding of what it was to be a leader. They knew their job, their goals and objectives, and the targets they had to hit, but not how to lead. I know now that I could have done the same interviews in many organizations and found similar results.

We reported our findings back to the board members and told them that the change programme would continue to stall unless we could create a consistent understanding of how to be a leader in their organization. They gave us the green light and off we embarked on the second programme.

Our challenge was to come up with a framework for leadership that was simple and effective, which we could roll out to around 600 managers. As we found out when we started our research, this wasn't the simplest of tasks. Most leadership frameworks we found were overly complicated. This was not about setting strategy or creating strategic priorities – that was done at the top of the organization and the directors were proficient in that. This was about middle and senior managers acting consistently to lead the organization forward to deliver on the strategy and the business plan. It was about clarity and alignment, two of the most important words in leadership.

Our research led us to a wonderfully simple framework created by Kouzes and Posner[2] that contains five leadership practices:

1. inspire a shared vision
2. model the way
3. challenge the process
4. encourage the heart
5. enable others to act.

This framework formed the basis of the programme we ran, and it has informed my thinking on leadership ever since.

As the years went by and I started to run more leadership programmes as well as coaching and speaking, I found that businesses needed a more substantial map of what leadership encompassed. The model I was using was brilliant, but I started to find other significant areas that were important

---

[2] James Kouzes and Barry Posner, *The Leadership Challenge*, 6th ed., 2017.

enough to be included. For example, the programme described above was focused around their core purpose, but the model had nothing on purpose – or, as some businesses call it, mission. I was starting to get involved in working more and more with leadership teams and there was little on building team excellence, motivation, happiness (positive psychology) and engagement. Finally I added a section I call 'show grit'. Working with CEOs and key executives showed me how gritty you must be to create and then build a successful business while maintaining a semblance of balance. The pressure of leading businesses, both large and small, is immense and unrelenting, and an understanding of grit and resilience is vital.

From my research and continuous work with leaders came the Leadership Map, a series of highly engaging workshops. I started running Leadership Map workshops with CEOs and executive groups across the United Kingdom and Ireland in 2018 and in the following two and a half years delivered it to over 700 leaders. It was very well received – so much so that in my first year I won Most in Demand New Speaker and in both the first two years of delivering the programme, I was awarded the Outperformer Award by Vistage UK.[3] This validation of the Leadership Map spurred me on to write the book, which in turn has made my workshops richer in their content.

---

[3] Vistage is the world's largest peer mentoring and coaching organization for CEOs, business owners and executives.

Leaders operate at every level in an organization; it's not the title on your card, it's the way you act that shows you are a leader.

The structure of the book

The Leadership Map has 12 areas that are shown in Figure I.1.

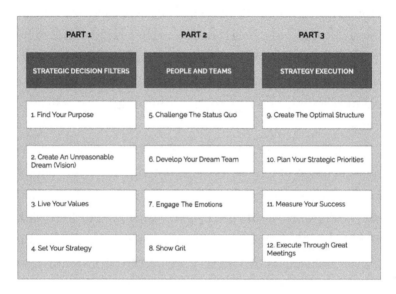

PART 1	PART 2	PART 3
STRATEGIC DECISION FILTERS	**PEOPLE AND TEAMS**	**STRATEGY EXECUTION**
1. Find Your Purpose	5. Challenge The Status Quo	9. Create The Optimal Structure
2. Create An Unreasonable Dream (Vision)	6. Develop Your Dream Team	10. Plan Your Strategic Priorities
3. Live Your Values	7. Engage The Emotions	11. Measure Your Success
4. Set Your Strategy	8. Show Grit	12. Execute Through Great Meetings

Figure I.1: The Leadership Map

The Leadership Map has three distinct areas, that form the three parts of this book:

- *Part 1: Strategic Decision Filters.* This shows you that the foundation of every business, once it moves beyond start-up, needs four critical areas. I call them strategic decision filters. When you have these in place, every decision you make becomes easier. When you work with your top team to create next year's strategic priorities, they must be in line with your purpose, your vision, your values and, of course, your strategy. Your people need to demonstrate how they live your values in their day-to-day actions. When your front-line staff deal with your customers, they need to understand your point of difference versus that of your competitors (strategy) and demonstrate your values (the behaviours you want to see) in everything they do and say.

- *Part 2: People and Teams.* As many great leaders have said, 'The most important thing a leader can do is to develop another leader.' This section is all about developing people and creating amazing teams. It starts with a journey into challenge, stretch and growth and describes how to create a business where this is part of the DNA. I then show how to develop high-performing teams based on a common purpose and goals, in the knowledge that it is safe to take a risk. The third area moves into happy and motivated workforces, looks at why this is essential and how it massively increases engagement and productivity. The final chapter in Part 2 looks at how to develop gritty, resilient people around you.

- *Part 3: Strategy Execution.* This final part starts with a look at what kind of organizational structure is most suitable for your business. It then describes a robust way of creating your strategic priorities. Next, you need to review and assess how you are doing through a 'dashboard' of key performance indicators (KPIs). These must be available in a comprehensive scorecard format that shows your top team, the financial information (which is historically based) and some predictors of future performance through KPIs on customers, your people and internal systems and processes. The final chapter in Part 3 is about the types of meetings you need to run and how to make them the best part of your day.

The final chapter of this book then addresses how to bring the whole Leadership Map together, integrating its tools into your business.

How to use this book

I had no intention of writing a book when I first created my Leadership Map programme. It was only when I first presented it that someone in the room said, 'Where's the book?' and I realized that I needed to write it all down. This process has forced me to think more deeply about the subject and, in turn, create better leadership programmes.

In each of the chapters, I have provided several tools that you can use in your business. At the end of each chapter, I ask five questions that will help you to decide how well you are leading in this area. When you use this tool, you will be able to see where you are strongest and where you need to improve. You can also subscribe to my newsletter, my blog and my podcast, *The Gritty Leaders Club*, which I co-host with Ben Wales (a great leadership coach and team builder).

My own purpose is to inspire leadership. This book is therefore designed to inspire *you* to become a better leader.

It is full of links to reference books, TED Talks, quotes and insights that I hope will help you to fulfil your leadership potential and to become the best leader you can be.

I'll leave you with ten key points to consider when you read this book and continue your journey to become a better leader:

1. *Leadership is never fully done.* Your aim should be to learn and improve every day. Leaders have a growth mindset.

2. *Leaders are visionaries.* In order to know what to do next month and next year, you need a vision of what you want your business to become and you must inspire your people to do everything in their power to achieve your vision.

3. *Leadership thrives on clarity and alignment.* Be very clear what you and your team stand for, what you want people to do and how they should behave, then align everyone around these core principles.

4. *Live the 80% rule.* You will never have all the information you need to make the call on the hard decisions you have to make. It requires risk-taking. So be bold and lean fully in.

5. *Leadership is half art and half science.* Know your tools and techniques, and critically consider how you will go about applying them in your business. All data are historical; creativity will make the difference in the future.

6. *It's not the title on your card that matters.* Leaders operate at every level in an organization, but it's the

way you act that shows you are a leader. Find out who your informal leaders – your influencers – are and develop them to create your future.

7. *Leaders are role models.* As a leader, you will be copied in everything you do, not what you say. Always think about the impact your actions are having.

8. *Leaders grow leaders.* One of the key components of leadership is to grow and develop others around you. Without doing that, you cannot achieve your goals.

9. *Leaders prioritize down-time and create balance in their lives.* Make sure you celebrate the good times at work and create an equally amazing personal life. Enjoy every part of the journey.

10. *Leaders don't have all the answers, but they do have great questions.* It is impossible to have all the answers for all the knotty challenges and opportunities that will come your way. Leaders show vulnerability and honesty, and ask others for their ideas and thoughts.

PART 1
Strategic decision filters

Chapter 1

Find your purpose

He who has a why to live for can bear almost any how.
– Friedrich Nietzsche

Introduction

I love this quote from Nietzsche and use it in both this chapter and in Chapter 8, but it is also relevant throughout most of *The Leadership Map*. It is just so true that with a very strong *raison d'être* – literally, 'reason for being' – much of what we do with our life becomes purposeful and decisions become easier to make and take. With a strong purpose that we believe in, we are determined to fulfil it by creating a vision, goals and plans to pursue it. When we come up against challenges, it gives us the resilience to overcome them because we simply must continue to fulfil our purpose.

In 2019, the New Zealand Rugby team (known as the All Blacks) arrived in Japan to play in the Rugby World Cup. The team had won the last two World Cups, back to back, and has the highest win rate of any national Rugby team in the world. The All Blacks are undoubtedly the most successful Rugby team ever. They have been called by many the most successful sports team ever! New Zealand is a country of 4.8 million people. Rugby in New Zealand isn't just a sport – a game of win or lose – it's a 'religion'! As James Kerr[1] says in his book *Legacy*, when you are facing the All Blacks you are facing a culture, an identity, an ethos, a belief system – and a collective passion and purpose beyond anything you have faced before. Many teams have lost before the game starts! It is undoubtedly hard to create this level of purpose in a business, but we can come close and we should try, because when our people have a purpose bigger than themselves that drives them to come to work, they will put their whole selves into achieving it.

The first chapter of *The Leadership Map* asks the simplest of questions: Why does your business exist? Organizations are about purpose, not place. As Tom Rath[2] has said, 'make work a purpose not a place'. When you find a purpose that inspires you, you want to be a part of it – you want to give your very best and you want others to do the same around you. Why does *your* business exist? This is a question that the founders of your business will have asked themselves when they put it together in the beginning. They may not have written it down, of course, because they just knew it and they all lived it, in every interaction with each other and with the early customers.

People are more concerned about finding meaning in their lives than ever before. The issue comes when we grow and start to recruit more people and they haven't got that automatic understanding of our 'why', as Simon Sinek so

---

[1] James Kerr, *Legacy: What the All Blacks Can Teach Us About the Business of Life*, 2013.

[2] Tom Rath is a Gallup senior researcher and author.

brilliantly put it in his TED Talk and book.[3] So we *do* need to write it down and we *do* need to communicate it. Why is this so important? Purpose is at the heart of every business and every individual. If we have a strong belief in what we do, we will be passionate about it and that passion will shine through in the way we say and do things. We will recommend our business to others who might be good enough to join us; we will demand more of our colleagues around us, because we care so much; and we will find it easy to sell, because it doesn't feel like selling – we are just telling people how good our products and services are.

We are also personally guided by our values and our motivational drivers, which allow us to decide what fits and what doesn't. Without these in place, it's hard to decide; it's hard to know what is right and what is wrong. In a business, we need the same mechanism to help our people make the right decisions because we know that the best businesses allow their people to make decisions at the front line, on their own, without referring to their boss. Purpose, along with vision, values and strategy are all strategic decision filters (Figure 1.1). Without all these in place and understood, where do you start in the annual setting of your strategic priorities? How do you know who to recruit or promote or fire, how to judge whether a prospect will likely make a great customer or whether to acquire a business?

---

[3] Simon Sinek's TED Talk, 'How Great Leaders Inspire Action', September 2009; Simon Sinek, *Find Your Why: A Practical Guide for Discovering Purpose for You and Your Team*, 2017.

Figure 1.1: Strategic decision filters

In 1999, Marcus Buckingham, part of the Gallup organization, wrote a book called *First Break All The Rules*.[4] This fascinating book is based on a comprehensive analysis of over one million employee interviews conducted over the previous decades. It shows that great managers do a number of key things really well:

- They focus on developing the strengths of employees, rather than addressing their weaknesses.
- They treat every individual differently.
- They challenge their employees to learn and grow.

The book outlines 12 questions that organizations can ask their employees. Answering 'yes' to these questions shows a

---

[4] Marcus Buckingham and Curt Coffman, *First Break All The Rules: What the World's Greatest Managers do Differently*, 1999.

high degree of engagement and productivity, and leads to greater creativity, job retention, customer satisfaction and profit. The 12 questions have become a well-used global staff survey tool, known as Gallup Q12.

It is clear from all the research that the 12 questions have been selected very carefully. Question 8 is 'Does the mission/purpose of my company make me feel that my job is important?' Business units in Gallup's top quartile on Q8 average from 5–15% higher productivity, have 30–50% fewer accidents and 15–30% lower staff turnover than those in the bottom quartile. Perhaps the key statement that came out of the research is that 'if a job is *just a job* it really wouldn't matter where someone worked'. The fact is that once basic needs are met, then employees search for a higher purpose in what they do. We will see this again in Chapter 7, when we look at motivation. Gallup has found that in highly engaged workforces it is not uncommon for employees to say that they have turned down higher paid jobs to gain more meaningful work. It is therefore crucial that managers throughout the organization really get the purpose of their business and can translate it into everyday working practices with their people.

Purpose in practice

Let me tell you a story that highlights the importance of a purpose – not only having one, but engaging your whole workforce in it. It's about Disney, whose purpose is 'creating happiness'.

Creating happiness: The Disney magic

A good friend of mine attended a leadership programme in Disney World, Florida, to learn some of the Disney magic that he could apply back in his business and with his clients.

During the lunch break one day, he and two of his colleagues were walking around the Park and taking in the sunshine. They decided it would be a good idea to take some selfies to remind them of the great trip they were having. A Disney employee was sweeping up some litter nearby and spotted them. She came straight over and asked them how their day was and if she could help them by taking some pictures of them together. Perfect they thought, and she snapped away.

They returned to the classroom in the afternoon and were greeted by the course director, who asked them how their lunch had gone. They told the story to the director, who smiled from ear to ear. "That's fabulous," she said. "I am so pleased to hear it. You see, at Disney we say to all our Cast Members (staff to you and me) that they have to be 'on purpose' for 100% of their time, but at times they can be 'off task'. What they cannot be is 'on task and off purpose'."

Disney describes its core purpose as 'A single unifying principle that connects every Cast Member with the emotional aspirations of our Guests'. Beautifully put, I think – and so simple to remember. When you write down your purpose, make sure that it is simple and memorable, like Disney's.

Let's look at a few more examples from businesses large and small, and from sport and business. We'll start with the amazing Southwest Airlines, established in 1966 by Rollin King and Herb Kelleher. Southwest has quite rightly been the subject of numerous business school case studies over the years, as an outstanding example of an enduring great company. An astonishing success story, the airline has 55,000 employees, over 700 Boeing 737s (it has only one type of aircraft to make its maintenance efficient) and flies to over 100 destinations. The airline's competitive strategy combines a high level of employee and aircraft productivity with low unit costs by reducing aircraft turn-around time, particularly at the gate. Many other low-cost airlines around the world have tried to copy Southwest's strategy, including easyJet and Ryanair in the United Kingdom.

One of the key differentiators in Southwest Airlines is the customer experience. Southwest offers free non-alcoholic in-flight drinks and alcoholic drinks are for sale at a flat rate of $5. The airline also offers free alcoholic drinks on popular holidays such as New Year's Day, Valentine's Day and Mardi Gras. If you visit YouTube, you will see numerous videos of Southwest cabin crew giving colourful and engaging boarding announcements with crews that burst out into song and some who even dance! One famous and very funny YouTube video went viral and the flight attendant, Martha Cobb, was invited onto the *Ellen DeGeneres Show* in the United States! What an amazing advertisement for the airline. As you will see in Chapter 3, Southwest Airlines really delivers on its purpose and values, and that must be one of the reasons it has remained profitable even in the economic downturns of the past 50 years.

Southwest can be seen to use its purpose as a decision filter. It has consistently refused to charge customers for checked bags, when most other low-cost carriers do. The airline would get an immediate injection of cash by doing so, but its purpose is 'To connect people to what's important in their lives through friendly, reliable and low-cost air travel'. Choosing not to charge customers for their bags is consistent with this purpose.

Virgin, founded by Sir Richard Branson and Nik Powell, started with a record shop and now operate a global conglomerate spanning everything from healthcare to banking to mobile phones, airlines and even commercial spacecraft. The two founders chose the name Virgin as they considered themselves 'virgins' in business – what a great success story! The annual revenue of the Virgin Group in 2020 was over £16.6 billion, employing almost 70,000 employees. Virgin Group's purpose is 'Changing Business for Good', an emotional statement that challenges everyone in their business. Virgin Group describe themselves as a 'family owned growth capital investor'. Virgin Group are known for challenging the status quo and disrupting industries. They are a very purpose-driven business who have stated that all their different businesses must have a clear purpose and use it when making business decisions.

One of the lessons that can be taken from Virgin Group is the idea of a group purpose being different from each of the different companies within the group. I am often asked when working with a large subsidiary if they should have a separate purpose (or vision, values or strategy) and my answer is 'it depends'. It depends on how different the business is. Ideally, you want as few of these decision filters as possible, so people in the business know what they are, what they mean and how to live them. Too many and it's too confusing, but at the same time they must reflect the business. In Virgin's case, if you work for Virgin Atlantic Airlines you will have a different purpose statement from other parts of the group. Virgin Atlantic's purpose, which it has called its mission, is 'To grow a profitable airline, that people love to fly and where people love to work'. It is no accident that Virgin Atlantic has put the word 'love' in twice. This powerful emotional word will inspire people in its business. In an interview in April 2019, Virgin Atlantic's CEO Shai Weiss said, 'We aim to be the most-loved travel company'. When developing your purpose, it must have that level of emotion in it.

Now from two huge businesses to a UK based SME – 48.3 Scaffold Design. This is a very successful business run by an exceptional entrepreneur, Ben Beaumont, with whom I've worked for several years now. When Ben came into the industry and decided to set up 48.3, he saw an industry with a history of health and safety issues, one where corners were cut and costs driven down. He says on his website, 'We've had enough of poorly conceived and cost-prohibited scaffold designs'. Ben has created a business with exceptionally talented people who focus on the design of complex scaffolding projects. 48.3 wants to 'transform sites into safe, efficient, risk-mitigated working areas'. Since that very first day, the company has driven the evolution of scaffolding design across the United Kingdom.

Creating your purpose

The first thing to say is that creating your purpose is messy, but messy doesn't mean it can't or shouldn't be done – indeed, to the contrary, it can and must be done. The question for many of us is how we create our purpose if we don't have one. Dan Buettner, a *National Geographic* Fellow and *New York Times* bestselling author, founded The Blue Zones. These are five places in the world where people live the longest and are the healthiest: Okinawa, Japan; Sardinia, Italy; Nicoya, Costa Rica; Ikaria, Greece; and Loma Linda, California. These five areas share nine lifestyle habits chronicled in his book *The Blue Zones*.[5] The second lifestyle habit of these long-living people is purpose. The Nicoyans call it *'plan de vida'* (literally life plan) and the Okinawans call it *Ikigai*. For both, it translates into 'why I get up in the morning'. The Blue Zones research shows that knowing your sense of purpose is worth up to seven years of extra life expectancy.

If you translate the Japanese characters of *Ikigai* (Figure 1.2), the first two characters mean 'life' and the second two characters mean 'to be worthwhile'.

IKIGAI

Figure 1.2: Ikigai

---

[5] Dan Buettner, *The Blue Zones: 9 Lessons for Living Longer from the People Who Live the Longest*, 2009.

A worthwhile life is what a purpose is all about, whether it be for an individual or a business. Oprah Winfrey said, 'You don't become what you want, you become what you believe.' So, start there – what do you believe? Another global success is the furniture retailer Ikea, which believes its purpose is 'To create a better everyday life for the many people'. BUPA, the UK private healthcare provider, believes its purpose is that people should have 'Longer, healthier, happier lives'. The purpose of TeamSport Indoor Go Karting, the no. 1 indoor go karting business in the United Kingdom is 'To create unique and exciting experiences for everyone'.

When you have a great purpose in your business, such as Disney's 'Creating happiness' or the All Blacks 'To add to the legacy', it will attract people to work for you, give them a framework to make better decisions – be they strategic or tactical – and keep them for longer. As the authors Héctor García and Francesc Miralles tell us in their book, *Ikigai,*[6] 'Our *Ikigai* is hidden deep inside each of us, and finding it requires a patient search.' The same is true in our organizations. If we are the founder, it may be clear to us, but being able to articulate it and write it down can sometimes be tricky.

The *Ikigai* model asks four questions that can be useful when figuring out your purpose:

1. What do you love?
2. What does the world need?
3. What can you be paid for?

---

[6] Héctor García and Francesc Miralles, *Ikigai: The Japanese Secret to a Long and Happy Life*, 2017.

4.   What are you good at?

Here are the first set of questions at the end of this chapter to help you understand how well you are doing when it comes to having a purpose and implementing it in your business.

Find your purpose

Questions for you and your leadership team

1.   Have you defined and written down your organizational purpose?
2.   Is your purpose clear and easy to understand?
3.   Are the members of your leadership team clear and completely aligned around your purpose?
4.   Do all your people understand your purpose?
5.   Do people use your purpose to make key decisions in the business? (Is it a 'decision filter'?)

Chapter 2

Create an unreasonable dream

The size of your dreams must always exceed your capacity to achieve them.

– Ellen Johnson Sirleaf

Introduction

After you find your purpose, a vision is the next most important thing to develop for your business. I am not talking about a vision statement – that's fine, but it needs to come out of something more tangible and meaningful and vivid. What you need to develop is a *descriptive vision*, one that paints a picture so clearly you can almost feel what it will be like in your business when you've achieved it. It is not written from the present – 'This is what we will achieve' – but from the future – 'This is what we have achieved'. I'll provide a tool to start you off in the development of such a vision with your top team at the end of this chapter.

Having established that your vision has to be descriptive, it must also be unreasonable. What do I mean by that? Well, if something is reasonable, it can be done now without a lot of effort – it's in your comfort zone. How compelling would that be? If you make it unreasonable, then it becomes energizing and exciting: you will have to do something different to get there. Your people must work out what that means for them and what they need to do differently to contribute to its achievement. Perhaps most importantly, it means that the business – and therefore your people – must stretch, learn and grow to get there. And when your people are stretching and growing, they are truly engaged in your business – as opposed to doing the same old thing, when they can become bored and disinterested.

I first used the expression 'unreasonable dream' when I was in the final practice for my TEDx Talk in November 2018. I was running through my 14-minute talk (which I had rehearsed until I was dreaming it!) in front of a panel in Woking in the United Kingdom. After I had finished, each member of the panel and the other speakers gave me feedback on what they thought went well and any ways they thought I could improve my presentation. Thankfully, the feedback was good and I progressed to the real thing (not everyone did progress – either they really didn't have 'an idea worth spreading'[1] or they just hadn't rehearsed enough). My original title was 'Self Discovery – the Real Legal High'. The TEDx Talk is about finding your purpose, creating your vision and stretching yourself to get there. One of the panellists spotted that I had referred to the importance of setting 'an unreasonable dream' in the talk. He said it was the standout phrase and

---

[1] TED is a non-partisan, non-profit organization, devoted to spreading ideas, usually in the form of short, powerful talks (18 minutes or less).

hooked him in – so it became the title of my TEDx Talk and has stayed with me ever since.

Unreasonable isn't just my opinion. Ellen Johnson Sirleaf was the first democratically elected woman of an African nation – Liberia. She had experienced a glittering career in the commercial world, with Citibank, the Equator Bank (part of HSBC) and the World Bank, before working in a variety of very senior roles in the United Nations, investigating the Rwandan genocide and the effect of conflict on women, and women's role in peacekeeping. Sirleaf was elected as Liberia's 24th President in 2006 and served through to 2018. She is an amazing woman who was awarded the Nobel Peace Prize in 2011 in recognition of her role in bringing women into the peacekeeping process. One of her quotes, which has inspired me, is 'The size of your dreams must always exceed your capacity to achieve them.' You must read it twice to really get it. It means, of course, that you need to develop and grow your capacity if you are going to achieve your dreams – you simply can't stand still. It's the thing that holds many people back. They discuss something they'd like to do or achieve, then they get stuck because they don't know how to achieve their goals today. Unreasonable dreams can't be achieved today with what you know now. They are inherently risky, you might not get there, there are no guarantees. But this is what separates the high achievers from the rest. They are prepared to go to new places, take a risk, stretch themselves, and learn and grow. I ended my TEDx Talk with an extract from a poem that I have on my bathroom wall at home. It inspires me every day and sums up my approach to life. It's by Marianne Williamson from her book *A Return to Love* and it was used in Nelson Mandela's inaugural speech in 1994.[2] It's called 'Our Deepest Fear'. The line in the poem that really spoke to me is, 'Your playing small does not serve the world'. That line challenges me every day to be the best I can be and to push myself to grow, reach my potential and achieve my vision to 'work with and inspire a million leaders'.

Vision in practice

On 25 May 1961, the US President, John F. Kennedy, announced to a joint session of the US Congress that before the end of the decade America would put a man on the moon and return him safely to earth. He asked Congress for an additional $9 billion (worth about $80 billion in 2020). So why was this vision such a great one? Well, it ticked many boxes:

1. *It lifted and engaged a nation.* The backdrop for Kennedy's vision to put a man on the moon was a nation in a bleak mood. The United States was starting to deploy troops into Vietnam (in what became a 10-year war) to fight off what they saw as the possible spread of communism throughout Asia. Kennedy had ordered the disastrous invasion of the Bay of Pigs to 'Liberate Cuba' from Castro in April of that year, which ended in failure. The Cold War was starting. Later that year, in August 1961, East Germany began the construction of the Berlin Wall, dividing East Germany from West Germany. In the United States, the Civil Rights

---

[2] Marianne Williamson, *A Return to Love: Reflections on the Principles of 'A Course in Miracles'*, 1997.

Movement was in full flow, dividing the country. We were only two years away from the famous 'I have a dream' speech delivered by Martin Luther King jr. to 250,000 people in Washington, DC. Russia had its own ambitions in space. On 12 April 1961, Yuri Gagarin became not only the first man in space, but the first to orbit the earth. Gagarin became a national hero of the Soviet Union and the Eastern Bloc, and a worldwide celebrity. The American nation was inspired, people's spirits were lifted. The United States was desperate to show the world what it could do.

2. *It was unreasonable.* This vision laid out by President Kennedy was probably the most famous unreasonable dream ever. When Kennedy made the speech, NASA must have felt massively challenged, if not a little scared, as it was so far away from developing the technology to put a man on the moon and bring him safely back to earth. The speech Kennedy gave the following year at the Rice University Football Stadium provided more clues as to why this was such a great vision. He challenged the American people, saying the United States was doing this 'not because it is easy, but because it is hard' and 'we intend to win'. As a leader, he set out his own agenda that he wanted people to follow. What he was saying was, 'If I can set such an unreasonable dream, then maybe in your lives you could too.'

3. *He inspired people.* Kennedy inspired a nation, and gave them hope and excitement about the future. He did this through some wonderful speeches, in which he shared his unreasonable dream and made himself

accountable for delivering on it. While it was audacious, the American people believed in him, and believed his dream could be achieved.

Remember Kennedy's words 'we do this not because it is easy, but because it is hard'. This vision – or unreasonable dream – was at the time impossible. It forced NASA to think differently and it inspired a nation. NASA figured out that it was no longer possible to achieve this vision by working harder or more hours; its people needed to move from comfort to stretch and to try new ways of doing things. On 20 July 1969, Apollo 11 did the impossible and touched down on the lunar surface, with 25 seconds of fuel left and 650 million citizens of the world watching on their black and white televisions and listening on their radios.

Organizational visions should follow these three principles of lifting up people's emotions, stretching them and inspiring them about what the business can do. If Kennedy had not created and shared such a vision, would NASA have landed a man on the moon in 1969? I think not. In fact, not a single one of the hundreds of CEOs to whom I have asked this question said it would have happened. What a powerful tool to have at your disposal as a leader! As I will say again and again in this book, great leaders need to focus more on asking great questions than on believing they have great answers. Look at the difference between these two questions that you could pose to your leadership team:

- We grew 10% last year and the economy looks like giving us no help this year. What would we have to do to maintain the same growth rate of 10%?

- We grew by 10% last year. What would we need to do differently to grow by 50% this year?

The first question will elicit no excitement and little stretch, and can rely only on marginal gains across the board. It also means staying in your comfort zone and trying little or nothing new, which can be very dangerous for a business. The second question is extremely challenging. It requires new thinking, perhaps new products or services, different types of people, new geographic markets, new features, new pricing, a refreshed brand and a new marketing push, and it brings energy, excitement and personal growth. That doesn't mean you will all agree on a 50% growth target, but from my experience, you'll end up with a commitment to much more than 10%.

Business vision

Let's now look at a business vision or two.

Amazon

Amazon has always had huge ambitions, driven by the extraordinary Jeff Bezos. Amazon has a mission (what I call purpose in Chapter 1) and a vision that it often puts side by side. Since Amazon's start in 1994 as a bookstore, Bezos quickly decided that it would be 'the earth's most customer centric company'. Amazon is, as Bezos has often said, 'customer obsessed'. Bezos's book *The Everything Store*[3] sums

---

[3] Jeff Bezos, *The Everything Store*, 2013.

up his vision in the title. He was never content to sell books: he wanted to sell 'anything customers want to buy online at the lowest possible prices'.

What I find special about this vision is that, like Kennedy's, it really stretches people. It's not just a vague statement like 'The *best* customer centric company'; Amazon says, '*the earth's most* customer centric company'. So now Amazon must judge its achievements against the best on the planet. It also needs to keep going until it stocks everything we'd want to buy online. As a decision filter, this makes it clear what Amazon must do:

- It must make it so easy and quick to do business with the company. I know that whenever I've had a problem with an Amazon product, it has been solved almost immediately and without a single quibble.
- It must keep expanding its online product range. What Amazon has achieved for most people is that it has become the place to *start* the online search, whatever you're looking for – whether it's a drinks fridge, a hot glue gun, an ethernet cable or yes, even books!

Tesla

Let's look at another vision from a company we keep hearing about that has been created by another extraordinary man, Elon Musk.

To create the most compelling car company of the 21st century by driving the world's transition to electric vehicles.

Founded in 2003, Tesla didn't turn a profit until the first quarter of 2014, something to which we will return in Chapter 8. Musk must be put into the category of people who are changing (or have changed) our world: Richard Branson, Benazir Bhutto, Winston Churchill, Rosa Parkes, Mahatma Gandhi, Nelson Mandela, Steve Jobs, Mother Teresa, Marie Curie and many more. They all had relentless ambition and an unreasonable vision of what could be achieved. Musk, who started with PayPal and then went on to build SpaceX and Tesla (he co-founded Tesla with four others, taking the controlling stake), can't keep off the front pages. The two original founders, Martin Eberhard and Marc Tarpenning, were influenced by the withdrawal from electric cars of GM with their EV1 car (another Kodak/digital camera moment that they must regret). The funding that Musk has brought into Tesla through his incredible ambition and grit to keep going, despite huge setbacks and near bankruptcy, has been nothing short of astonishing. Toyota and Daimler own 10% each, Google co-founders Sergey Brin and Larry Page are investors and the US Department of Energy has provided low-interest loans.

For Tesla, Musk's vision is to eventually bring electric cars to the world.

There will be future cars that will be even more affordable down the road... With fourth generation and smaller cars and what not, we'll ultimately be in a position where everyone can afford the car.

– Elon Musk at the Future Transport Solutions conference, Oslo, 21 April 2016

SpaceX

Let's briefly turn to SpaceX, another Elon Musk-owned business that is changing the world. The company was founded in 2002 with the goal of enabling people to live on other planets. Its mission is to 'enable humans to become a spacefaring civilization and a multi-planet species by building a self-sustaining city on Mars'.

Mind mental health charity

Visions apply to every type of business – large and small. Mind is a mental health charity in the United Kingdom with a bold vision that states, 'We won't give up until everyone experiencing a mental health problem gets both support and respect.'

Mind has real passion and conviction about it. I love the fact that they 'won't give up', and of course with more attention being given to mental health globally, this charity's work is in huge demand.

IKEA

A final example from the world of the large corporates is IKEA. This incredible company really has developed a unique place in the marketplace globally. Its vision is 'A better everyday life for the many people'. I love this vision statement because it has real clarity of purpose; there is real emotion running through the statement, which drives the people in that business.

TeamSport Indoor Go Karting

I spend much of my time now working with CEOs and their leadership teams in SMEs in the United Kingdom. TeamSport Indoor Go Karting is the no. 1 indoor go karting business and has grown dramatically under the leadership of Dominic Gaynor. In 2020, it had 35 tracks across the United Kingdom and set a new bold vision:

> *To be a leading leisure brand with 50 venues, internationally, by 2022.*
>
> *– TeamSport Indoor Go Karting*

Unfortunately, as for many businesses, the Coronavirus pandemic struck in early 2020 and the timing of TeamSport's vision has had to be pushed back, but the determination to get there remains undiminished. The interesting thing about TeamSport's vision is that it moved from an aspiration to be the no. 1 indoor go karting business to 'being a leading leisure brand'. Notice how this broadened the focus of the business and allowed it to develop new offerings for its customers. In 2019, it developed Putt Club, an indoor nine-hole, motorsport-themed indoor putting course. Prior to that, TeamSport had introduced Laser Quest and climbing walls in some of its venues. By changing its vision (once it had achieved its original goal), TeamSport created a new decision filter that allowed it to widen its strategic scope.

As you move through the pages of this book, you will see that every chapter can be applied not only to business but also to your personal life. You must find your own purpose and write it down, and you must also set yourself an unreasonable dream.

So let's look at an individual who started with an unreasonable dream and has created an extraordinary life: Arnold Schwarzenegger. He was born in Austria after World War II to a father who was chief of police in the town of Thal. He loved sports and started lifting a barbell in a gym when he was 15 years old. From an early age, he dreamed big and wanted more. He went to the local cinema in Graz, where he trained, watching his idols, Reg Parks, Steve Reeves and Johnny Weissmuller, who were professional body builders and actors. This is where he crafted his personal vision to move to the United States and became a body building professional. Just think about this: it was totally unreasonable, he couldn't speak English and at the time he was only just starting his body-building journey.

Arnold spent a year in the Austrian army, where he won his first body-building competition. From there he progressed to European body-building competitions before being spotted in London and moving to the United States. At the age of 20, he won the Mr Universe title before going on to win Mr Olympia seven times.

But body building was only the start of his career and his dream. Living in Los Angeles, he began to mix with influential people in films and he decided that he wanted to get into acting. He was told early on that it just wouldn't happen – he was too big, and he had a ridiculous accent that nobody would understand. Yet he turned both into positives in his acting career. In 1977, he was in what became a cult black and white movie about body building called *Pumping Iron*.

Then his big breakthrough came with *Conan the Barbarian* in 1982, followed by a series of action blockbusters including *The Terminator*, *Total Recall* and *Twins*. In the late 1980s, as his interest in politics grew, he announced himself as a Republican supporter and in 2003 he finally became Governor of California. In 2006, he was elected for a second term in office. What an astonishing achievement by a small boy from Austria!

Your vision is a decision filter

A vision is one of your company's decision filters (along with purpose, values and strategy). Without a compelling vision, how do you know how to set your strategic priorities, goals and targets for the following year? In other words, without a clear destination, you are just as likely to take the wrong road.

In a start-up business, the vision is likely to be in the mind of the founder and probably not written down. When you grow and there is a requirement to bring more people in, you need to write down and engage your people in your vision. A vision is for the CEO and the top team to craft and then bring to life for the business's people. It's then the organization's challenge to work out how it will be achieved.

Creating your vision

If you need to create a vision from scratch, or to recreate one (as a time-bound vision will need to be recrafted as you approach achievement), give your leadership team the following challenge:

- It's three years from now (provide an exact date). You are celebrating the achievement of your vision with the whole company.
- You are going to deliver a speech to everyone saying how you achieved the vision and what the company did to get there. Give them a set of criteria to base their speech around. Decide which elements of the following you want to include: business growth, turnover, earnings before interest, tax, depreciation and amortization (EBITDA), clients, partnerships, your people, culture, new products and services, marketing and sales, new markets, etc.
- Write this speech based on your understanding of what you need to achieve over the coming years and read it out at your next management meeting.

When the team members read out their speeches, you will see how ambitious they are, how aligned you all are and the level of detail they have gone into. This will allow you to pull together a vision that you can all buy into, because you have all been a part of the process. The speech can be about their part (division, department or region) of the business or the business as a whole. Some founders and CEOs have a very clear idea of their vision and want to craft it themselves and present it to the top team (in which case, ask the leadership team to do the exercise for their part of the business). Other CEOs want to co-create the vision with their team. In my experience, this creates the best visions with the most buy-in.

Your vision cannot be just a financial target. A stretching financial growth target (what Jim Collins refers to as a Big

Hairy Audacious Goal, or BHAG) by a given date is of course needed for the owners and the leadership team, but on its own is unlikely to engage your workforce. So you need both: an emotional, stretching, clear vision for everyone, underpinned by a financial goal for your shareholders and the leadership team.

The next thing you need to do is to bring the vision to life for your organization. This isn't easy, but just reading out a vision statement is unlikely to be that inspiring and it will be open to interpretation. You need to write a creative document to bring it to life and allow your people to 'stand in the vision'. This document will describe in some detail what it will look like when you have achieved your vision. This document needs to pull together all the speeches from your top team, from every angle.

At the end of this process, you should aim to have two documents:

1. a detailed vision document that describes the business in three years' time
2. a vision statement that captures the essence of the longer document and is often used on your website and shared with the outside world.

Now you have created clarity and alignment, not only in your top team, but with your organization. What your people now need to know is what they need to do to get there. Your detailed three-year vision will need to be reviewed on an annual basis (or sooner if an event throws your planning into chaos, as the Coronavirus did in 2020).

Create an unreasonable dream

Questions for you and your leadership team

1. Do you have a clear, stretching and detailed vision that describes what your business will look like in three years' time?
2. Is your vision up to date and was it created or refreshed with input from your leadership team?
3. Has everyone in your business been engaged in your vision, not only when launched, but regularly since?
4. Do you create opportunities as a leadership team to talk about your vision, both internally and externally?
5. Do you use your vision as a 'decision filter' when creating your annual strategic priorities and when making critical decisions throughout the year?

Chapter 3

Live your values

It's the way we do things around here.

Introduction

Arguably the most important part of a business is its culture. 'Culture' is one of those words that is difficult to define in a business. The best definition I have come across was from a global business that operates out of the south coast of England, called WDS Global. I was fortunate to work with them on their culture for several years. Their definition was simple: 'It's the way we do things around here.' I refer to culture in several chapters as it is made up of so many components.

So who sets the standards? Where do these 'things' emanate from? All my experience shows me that it starts with the leadership team. Culture succeeds or fails from the top. Simply put, leaders have to role model the values and behaviours that they expect of others in the business. Where did the values come from originally? Well, the founders of the organization will have established the business by living them and the first few employees will have seen how the founders acted and followed their lead. When the business grows, this becomes more and more of a problem. First the leadership team grows, then the 'front line' grows in numbers and then a layer of middle management is established to manage the front line.

The senior leadership team must look for opportunities to role model the values of the business and show them in action. Clarity and alignment are crucial. It is unnecessary to write down the values in the first few years, as everyone is often working in the same room and the business operates like a family. However, as the business grows it is important to agree about exactly what the values are (and mean) and what the behaviours are that follow each of the values. These must be crystal clear, open to no interpretation and followed to the letter from the top. If one member of the top team 'goes rogue', then you might as well not have them. When they are crystal clear, it is easy to say, 'Those are our values and you are, or you are not, living them.' Without them being written down, that is difficult or impossible.

One of the exceptional businesses with which I have worked over many years is an IT support and managed services provider called ramsac.[1] The culture of the business is central to everything it does, and every year it produces a 'ramsac culture book' for anyone to see. This culture book is made up of unedited testimonials from the company's employees, describing what it means to work at ramsac and to be part of team ramsac. What a fantastic thing to be able to do! It is a great recruitment tool and is something ramsac wants all potential recruits to read before attending an interview. It is not surprising that this business has won numerous awards for its culture and leadership.

---

[1] See www.ramsac.com.

The behaviours required of your employees (from the values) are one of three key parts of any performance management (appraisal) programme:

1. the objectives and targets you have agreed to deliver over an agreed timespan (in line with the organization's strategic priorities, and often running for a year)
2. the values and behaviours you agree to live by (in line with the organization's values)
3. a personal development plan to grow you as an individual.

Without clearly articulated values, no one can be held to account for not acting in the 'right way'. An important point to make here is that you must recruit people who already live your values, so that your values are reinforced by new members of staff, not challenged by them. I will describe 10 ways in which values can be reinforced in a business at the end of this chapter.

Good and bad values

So, what do a good set of values look like and how do you create them? Let's start with the principles that need to be considered when creating or refreshing your values:

1. *The number of values.* The fewer the better is a good principle. The best organizations have between three and five. The big problem with more than that is being able to remember what they are. I've come across some companies that have 10 or more values,

with long descriptions for each. These always appear to have been developed by consensus from the top team or perhaps HR or marketing, and have a variety of words mixed up in the descriptions so that they don't 'miss anything out'.

2. *Your wording.* The wording should reflect how you talk to each other in your business. A tech company in Silicon Valley will speak differently from a bank in London. The way the values are stated and described should therefore be different. I always think that any value on its own could quite easily belong to another company, but the combination (your recipe) of your values should be quite unique to you.

3. *The description.* There must be real clarity in the words you use, as the last thing you want is individual interpretation. For example, a one-word value such as 'security' could be interpreted in different ways – for example, taking care of your people or a padlock and chains. So if you have one-word values, you then need a description underneath each one that makes it very clear what they mean. Some businesses choose to write their values as short descriptions, in a few words that need no explanation. These are my favourites, as not only are they clear, but they also allow you to use words that are common in your business and show how you are different. The best organizations are transparent with their values and show them on their website. They will talk about them with their customers, partners and suppliers and look for a 'fit' when they make the choice to work with them.

Examples of great values

It still amazes me how many businesses don't understand either the importance of values or how to create them. Too many seem to have been created by committee. The result is too many values, written in corporate speak that no one in the business fully understands. Quite frankly, it would be better not to have them at all. Let's look at a few good examples where organizations have got it right.

Southwest Airlines has three great values:

1. Warrior Spirit
2. Servant's Heart
3. Fun LUVing Attitude.

You can see how unique these are. They convey a different culture straight away and they shout out what is important to Southwest. The other thing about great business values is that they should evoke an emotional feeling. These brilliant values have emotion running right through them. If you take a look at YouTube, you will find videos showing these values in action. In 2014, a flight attendant called Martha Cobb was recorded delivering a brilliant in-flight safety briefing that was posted on YouTube. It started with 'I'd like to *pretend* to have your attention for just a few moments.' It went viral on YouTube (as of July 2020 it had 25 million views) and got so much attention that she was invited onto *The Ellen deGeneres Show* in the United States. Just imagine what that did for Southwest Airlines bookings! Southwest encourages its staff to really live its values every day, and every year it rewards those who have demonstrated that they have lived them. I will mention Southwest Airlines a few times throughout the book, as it is such a great case study of a business that does things well.

Let's look at a small to medium enterprise (SME) in the United Kingdom. TeamSport Indoor Go Karting (already mentioned in Chapter 2) is the number one indoor go karting business in the United Kingdom. With the fast growth the business has achieved over the last few years, it has been so important to recruit and retain great people, and TeamSport's values and culture have been central to that.

The TeamSport values are lived in every one of its tracks, are central to its performance management system and proudly sit on the company website. You will immediately see how they have been worded to reflect the kind of business TeamSport is in:

We...

1. Put the customer on pole
2. Are one crew
3. Stand up and stand out
4. Have a big emphasis on small details
5. Are fuelled by fun.

As you can see, these are short phrases that need no explanation.

Let's look at one more example: Toyota. The Toyota Way is how every Toyota employee must behave, whether in manu-facturing or sales and marketing. The Toyota Way is a total management philosophy. When I worked as a consultant with Toyota and Lexus in the early 2000s, the unwritten rule was, 'It says Toyota on the door'. In other words, this is how you must be. Every meeting I ever attended in Toyota lived the company's values and as a result the culture and alignment of Toyota's people is phenomenal. Toyota has a small book that describes its values in detail, including the historical connections and stories that bring them to life. Toyota's values are:

1. Continuous improvement
   - Challenge
   - *Kaizen*
   - *Genchi Genbutsu*

2. Respect for people
   - Respect
   - Teamwork.

These five values fit under two pillars and are central to the Toyota culture. Each value must be understood and acted upon by individuals. Promotion in Toyota is only achieved by those performing at their best and living the values; the two are inextricably linked.

The first value of challenge sets the tone for those working in or working with Toyota. The company is challenging because it sets such high standards of excellence. The company challenges itself and everyone with whom it works to constantly learn and improve (see *Kaizen*). Then we have the two Japanese words *Kaizen* and *Genchi Genbutsu*, which require translation as well as explanation. *Kaizen* is all about continuous improvement, driving for innovation and evolution. Central to *Kaizen* is a growth mindset of organizational learning.

Genchi Genbutsu is a little more complicated. In Toyota, you must always 'go see for yourself and truly understand the situation'. Only with all the facts can you possibly make the right decision. Coupled with this is something called *Nemawashi*, or consensus building. Effective consensus building without rushing is critical to this value, as it allows you to gauge all the opinions of the stakeholders. Then, when you decide to implement, you can be confident enough to move rapidly.

The second pillar is respect for people. Respect means that employees make every effort to respect each other and take individual responsibility to build trust through honest and 'sincere' communication. Finally, teamwork acknowledges the power of the team: how members share opportunities for development and commit to learning. There is no doubt that my experiences of working with Toyota and Lexus over long periods of time showed me that they take their values more seriously than most other businesses with which I have worked. Professor Jeffrey K. Liker's book *The Toyota Way*[2] has a quote on the front cover that sums up Toyota well:

> *Toyota is as much a state of mind as it is a car company.*
> – USA Today

Creating your values

When creating your values, it is vital to put in the time and bring together the right people. However, before we get into

---

[2] Jeffrey K. Liker, *The Toyota Way*, 2004.

the creation, let's look at the types of values you should and shouldn't have. Values must be developed from the behaviours that are lived in your business today, not what you'd like to be in the future. You'll notice that people in your business do live your values – just not every day in everything they do. The challenge is to make them simple enough to remember, clear in the way they are written (not ambiguous) and not too numerous. In Patrick Lencioni's book, *The Advantage*,[3] he talks about 'permission to play' values. These are what too many companies start with, like honesty and integrity. I agree with Lencioni that these should be a given in your business and are not something you need to put in your list of values.

Jim Collins and Jerry Porras, in their book *Built to Last*,[4] define core values as being inherent and sacrosanct. These are the values that you want all your people to live in the way they interact with each other internally and with your customers externally. Core values are already lived within your business, just not by everyone and not consistently all the time. It is therefore possible to see them in action, write them down and share them. You know who the people are who are living them. I regularly ask people in organizations to think of the best person they know who lives their values and it's easy for them to tell me who that person is. It might be the person on reception, a director, a founder or a sales

---

[3] Patrick Lencioni, *The Advantage: Why Organizational Health Trumps Everything Else in Business*, 2012.

[4] Jim Collins and Jerry Porras, *Built to Last: Successful Habits of Visionary Companies*, 1994.

executive. The interesting thing is that everyone knows who they are.

Over the years as a consultant, I have used different techniques to help organizations create their unique set of values, but the one I now use is so obviously right that I am sure I will use it from here on. Here's how to create your values. Bring together your senior leadership team (there should be no abstentions) along with several people from different parts of the business. These should be key influencers – people who make a difference and are already well respected. Make sure you allocate around four hours for this first session. Ideally, you want around 12+ in the room (preferably in teams of four on separate tables) with an external facilitator (the key thing is that you cannot take part and facilitate the session at the same time). You need an initial hour or so to show people why you are creating values, what good values look like, what you will use them for in the business and what the role of leadership is in role-modelling them. When everyone is on the same page, you can then start the creative process. Here are the steps:

1. Everyone needs to think of someone in the business (they might be in the room but this is not essential) who they believe lives the values wholeheartedly. This sounds like an odd request when you don't have a set of values yet, however, everyone knows who this person is! Now, once everyone has someone in mind (the person's name is not to be shared), they need to write down the behaviours they exhibit everyday (up to six behaviours).

2. Everyone now shares the behaviours they have written down in their sub-teams and collates all the behaviours into one list on their table. Ask them to try to restrict the number they have in each sub-team table to around six. They will probably end up with a few more and that's okay for now.

3. The facilitator should now ask each sub-team in turn to write the six behaviours on a flip chart. There will be lots of overlap between the sub-teams.

4. Now comes the messy business of turning the three flip charts into one flip chart and agreeing on a few well-written value descriptions.

It is unlikely that you will finish this work on the day. Every session I have run with a top team has then been left for a few days so everyone can reflect on the list. Someone should then be held accountable to complete the work of wordsmithing the list, which can then be agreed by the leadership team.

Implementing and embedding values

Now you have done half the work. Implementation and embedding are next. Here are 10 steps to follow:

1. *Engaging the business.* The first step is to tell everyone in your business that you have a new set of values and how you came to create them. It is important that people know that you involved a team in their creation and that the exercises involved considering

how the best exemplars from your business behave today. Often businesses do the engagement in an 'all hands' meeting, and many with which I have worked combine this with rolling out a new vision, goals and strategy. Putting them all together in one engagement is often useful, as it allows people to see how they all fit together.

2. *Hiring and induction.* Many companies now hire first on values and second on experience and job fit. The easy part, in a way, is to establish whether a person has the right background and experience. It is much harder to work out whether a person fits your values. My first career was spent in the Foreign and Commonwealth Office in London and for many years in a number of capitals around the world. In my later years, I headed up a large part of the recruitment department. I brought in assessment centres in the early 1990s and professionalized the recruitment process. One of the things I still remember well is that 'the best predictor of future behaviour is past behaviour'. That's not to say we can't change, but our values and beliefs are less likely to change as they are embedded at an early age – some research suggests even by the age of five. Make sure that you design your questions (behavioural questioning) based around how people went about achieving their past goals and objectives as well as what they achieved.

3. *Performance management (appraisals).* When I started my first job, appraisal interviews were something done begrudgingly once or twice a year at best. They

were seen as a tick box exercise. Now the best organizations will have weekly sit-down talks between line manager and staff and more formal meetings once a month. The two-way conversation needs to cover how you are progressing against your objectives and targets, how you are developing and growing your capabilities and how well you are living your values. Both parties should prepare to discuss how well the person being appraised is living the values of the business, using specific and recent examples. Broadbrush feedback is useless and is lazy leadership. What the person needs is to know exactly what they did and how it did or didn't fit with the way the company wants their people to operate. If people are off track, it must be pointed out early so adjustments can be made.

4. *Website.* If you're proud of your values, then put them on your website. If you search around, you will find examples of values on the websites of most successful companies in the world, from Apple and Microsoft to SMEs in your local community. As a decision filter, those wishing to work for you as well as those who want to be your suppliers or customers should be able to find out what you stand for.

5. *Social media.* When people are searching out details about your company, they are likely to be looking on social media to see what is being said about you and what you are saying about yourself. This is not to say that you will necessarily keep talking about what your values are; rather, you should be telling stories

about what you are doing that demonstrates your values in practice. Give people a sense of what it would be like to work for you. As with all marketing channels, you must be using video. According to Zenith (part of Publicis Media), the average person will spend 100 minutes per day watching online video in 2021.

6. *Advertising and PR.* People read articles that interest them, and our attention spans seem to decrease year on year. If something doesn't grab you in the first sentence, chances are you will turn off and put it down. When I did my research on what makes a good TED Talk, I found out that they are largely formed of stories, not facts and figures. People love a good story, and that's how to engage your audience and bring your values to life.

7. *Internal communications.* The global Coronavirus pandemic has accelerated our use of video technology. The best organizations were already using video to communicate with their people, and if you can't do it face to face, it is the next best way. Everyone in your business needs to know what your purpose is, what your unreasonable dream (your vision) is, what your strategy (competitive advantage) is and what your values (the way you behave) are. This isn't a one-off exercise; as the CEO of a marketing agency once told me, 'Communication should be irrigation not flood.' Your people need frequent updates,

reminders, success stories and energy from the leadership team, and your values must be woven through these messages.

8. *Succession planning.* Like recruitment, succession planning discussions must involve not only how well someone is hitting their targets, but how they are going about it. As people progress further up an organization, they are more frequently in the spotlight and must be seen to role model the values.

9. *Reward.* There are many ways to reward people in organizations. Annual award ceremonies are great occasions to give awards to the people in your business who go the extra mile to live your values. Companies like Breathe, which specializes in HR software for SMEs, have a system built into their software called Kudos, which allows peer-to-peer nomination for doing something outstanding. If you are going to be serious about values, then show you value the people who demonstrate them.

10. *Firing people.* When people are not living your values, they must be 'removed from the bus', to use Jim Collins' phrase. The question to ask yourself is whether you think you've kept people for too long who haven't lived your values, or you have got rid of them too early. I know what your answer will be. Don't hang on to people who are not living your values; it will erode your credibility as a leader.

Live your values

Questions for you and your leadership team

1. Do you have a clear set of values for your business that are written down?
2. Are your values words or phrases? If they are one-word values, are there clear descriptions written and understood for each of them?
3. Were your values created in an inclusive way, with people from within your business as well as your leadership team?
4. Have your values been rolled out and discussed with everyone in your business?
5. Are your people held accountable for living them?

Chapter 4

Set your strategy

The essence of strategy is choosing what not to do.
— Michael Porter

Introduction

When I start running a strategy session with a leadership team, I always kick it off with the question 'What is strategy?' After a few minutes of personal reflection, I ask everyone to give me their answers, which I write up on a flip chart – business leaders generally find the word 'strategy' confusing. When I first studied strategy at business school in 1993, it was all about Michael Porter, who gave us some real clarity about what strategy was and the importance of strategy in giving us a competitive advantage. Since then, many people have talked about strategy when they mean other things. When I type 'strategy' into Google, I get 3.7 million results! The most common response I get from audiences is that a strategy is a plan to achieve your vision, but that's not strategy – that's your strategic priorities or goals over a timeline.

Let's start with Michael Porter from his 1985 seminal book *Competitive Advantage*.[1] Porter talked about 'three generic strategies':

---

[1] Michael Porter, *Competitive Advantage*, 1985.

1. differentiation
2. cost leadership
3. focus.

Porter said you must be very clear about which one of these you follow, otherwise you could be 'stuck in the middle' with no competitive advantage. When customers compare products and services, they look for differences in, for example, quality or price or features.

If we now travel 16 years further forward and look at another luminary of leadership, Jim Collins, he talks about the hedgehog concept.[2] The hedgehog concept simplifies this model, saying that we need to look at three things:

1. what we really love to do (what we are deeply passionate about)
2. what we can be the best in the world at
3. how we make money (our economic engine).

Collins tells us that if we want the core of our business to be great (as opposed to just good), then we must be the best in the world at something, although to be fair he describes this model as 'an understanding', not a strategy. Collins' research in his book *Good to Great* gives us some interesting findings:

1. Good to great companies are more like hedgehogs – simple creatures that know 'one big thing' and stick to it. The comparison companies are more like foxes

---

[2] Jim Collins, *Good to Great*, 2001.

– crafty, cunning creatures that know many things yet lack consistency.

2. There is no evidence that good to great companies spent more time on strategic planning.

3. You don't have to be in a great industry to produce sustained great results.

If we now move another 18 years forward and look at the *Harvard Business Review* on 17 October 2018, Professor Kevin Boudreau gives us a four-step process in his 'Strategy for Entrepreneurs' article.[3] When we consider these three models, they are all slightly different, but have areas in common. Boudreau says there are four critical areas we must understand:

1. our customers
2. the problem we are solving
3. how we make money
4. how we are different.

Strategy in practice

There are numerous versions of strategy models out there, but I find them either too complicated to interpret or too simplified. In Figure 4.1, I have combined the key elements of many of the models I have found and put them into an easy-to-use structure.

---

[3] Kevin Boudreau, 'Strategy for Entrepreneurs', *Harvard Business Review*, 17 October 2018.

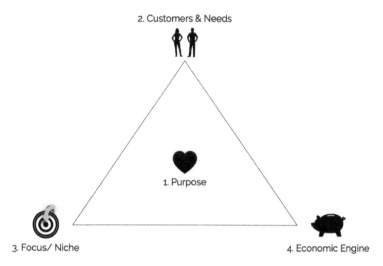

Figure 4.1: The strategy triangle

The four elements look like this:

1. *Our purpose.* We must start with our purpose, what we truly believe in and are passionate about.
2. *Our customers and their needs.* We need to be very clear about who our customers are and what their needs are. We cannot and should not try to sell to everyone.
3. *Our focus or niche.* This is our point of difference, where we are unique and, as Jim Collins says, where we can be world class. Our focus or niche is the critical part of this model. There are three areas where we can be world class:
   - operational excellence (cost leadership)
   - product leadership (superior products)
   - customer intimacy (personalization).

If we look at supermarkets in the United Kingdom, we can see clearly where their focus lies:

- *Operational excellence.* The German brand Aldi founded in 1913 in Essen has focused heavily on operational excellence. Aldi entered the UK market in 1990 and slowly gained a foothold, eroding the space occupied by Tesco. By early 2020, Aldi operated almost 900 stores across the United Kingdom. Aldi has no interest in making the customer experience a great one and their customers have no expectations that they will. It keeps its costs (and hence prices) low, sells mainly exclusive own-brand products sourced from local producers and offers a limited range. Aldi's biggest competitor in the United Kingdom is now Lidl, another German discount supermarket chain following a similar strategy.
- *Product leadership.* Whole Foods Market is an American supermarket chain established in 1990 with stores in the United Kingdom, Canada and the United States. The company's mission is to 'Promote vitality and well-being of all individuals by supplying the highest quality, most wholesome foods available'. One of Whole Foods Market's core values is 'selling the highest quality natural and organic products'. It is very clear how the company's core values and mission drive its strategy. Its product strategy is clear, focusing on natural and organic foods to attract discerning individuals and families.

- *Customer intimacy.* The UK supermarket chain Waitrose is part of the John Lewis partnership. Waitrose's aim is to be everything the discounters are not, through a focus on service, range and delivering an enjoyable customer experience. A Waitrose store has much wider aisles than its competitors, staff are trained to a higher level and will take you to the produce you are asking for and the chain offers free takeaway coffee and newspapers for MyWaitrose customers.

While each of these competitors has a clear point of difference (competitive advantage) (Figures 4.2 and 4.3) in their chosen area, they must also deliver a minimum standard on the other two areas. You could never accuse Waitrose of having poor products or lacking in operational efficiency – it is just not their competitive advantage.

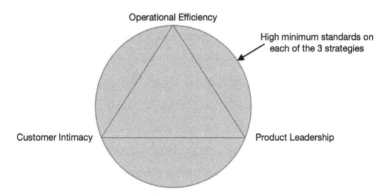

Figure 4.2: Creating your point of difference I

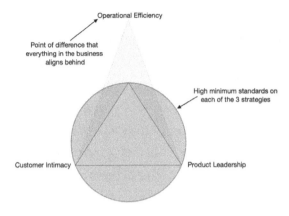

Figure 4.3: Creating your point of difference II

4. *Our economic engine.* Finally, how do we make money? What kind of margin are we looking at? Are we looking at selling lots of units at a lower price point and a lower margin or are we looking at few units at a higher price point and a higher margin?

Let's take this model and apply it to a few well-known companies. We will start with IKEA, which has a focus on operational efficiency (Figure 4.4).

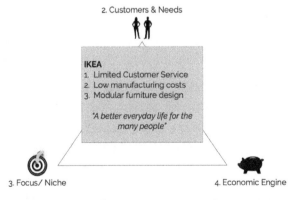

Figure 4.4: The strategy triangle – IKEA

IKEA's purpose is to create 'A better life for the many people'. Its customers are a combination of students and mainly middle-class people who are looking for nicely designed, good value products (and are happy to self-assemble). IKEA's focus or niche is a combination of modern, modular furniture design, high levels of stock on site and limited customer service – the key is operational efficiency, a strategy that gives IKEA a competitive advantage. Recently my wife and I decided we wanted a kitchen island to give us more work surface in our kitchen. What we found through IKEA was that they offered a terrific service. A first Zoom call established our needs and the customer service agent designed our island to our specifications. This was followed by a trip to our local store, where the design was completed and interior features were chosen. IKEA's customer service was there when we wanted it (to a high minimum standard), but it isn't their point of competitive advantage, which is founded on operational efficiency.

Let's start with operational efficiency and a company we've looked at before: Southwest Airlines, founded in 1967 by Herb Kelleher (Figure 4.5). In March 2020, Southwest was the world's second biggest airline by market value, and the world's largest low-cost airline, even though it served only the United States and Mexico. That, of course, is part of its secret: focus. In 2019, Southwest carried 134 million passengers and in December 2018 the CEO, Gary Kelly, announced an annual net profit of $3.5 billion, which was the 45th straight year of profits. That is astonishing when you consider the economic crashes that the airline industry has had to endure, from oil crises to financial crises.

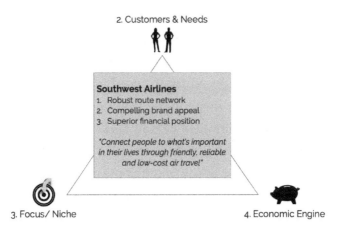

Figure 4.5: The strategy triangle – Southwest Airlines

Southwest Airline's purpose is 'To connect people to what's important in their lives through friendly, reliable, low-cost air travel'. Its vision is to be 'The world's most loved, most efficient and most profitable airline'. Put these two together and you get a very clear filter to make all the key decisions that are needed in the business.

Southwest's customers are predominantly business travellers and families looking for value. The airline's focus or niche sets it apart from many airlines: Southwest's planes fly point to point and it does not operate on the hub and spoke system that most airlines have adopted. Southwest has always used one type of aircraft – the Boeing 737 – to keep costs down on parts and service, and does not regularly codeshare with other airlines, which allows it to protect its brand. Southwest's customer service is quirky and encourages staff to not take themselves too seriously. As I discussed in Chapter 3, there are many YouTube videos showing amazing examples of inflight announcements that are funny, engaging and very different.

Finally, Southwest's economic engine is run on low costs, high utilization (volume) and quick turnaround of planes.

Let's now move to product leadership as a strategy. Dyson is a British technology company started in 1991 by Sir James Dyson. Dyson's first breakthrough product was his bagless vacuum cleaner. In the shed behind his house, Dyson developed 5127 prototype designs between 1979 and 1984 before he got it right. Dyson famously said that meant there were 5127 failures! Dyson's first success came with the DC01 vacuum cleaner, which became the biggest selling vacuum cleaner in the United Kingdom in just 18 months. By 2001, the DC01 made up 47% of the upright vacuum cleaner market.

To be product led and create the clear competitive advantage that Dyson has means continuous investment in research and development (R&D) (Figure 4.6). The line of successful products Dyson has brought to market over the years – hand dryers, hair dryers and stylers, fans and lighting – is only half the story. The company invested in many products that haven't (yet) been brought to market, including household robots, a Dyson chair and most famously a Dyson electric car.

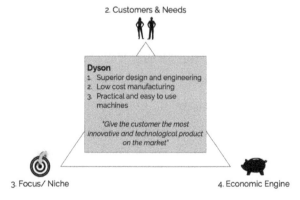

2. Customers & Needs

Dyson
1. Superior design and engineering
2. Low cost manufacturing
3. Practical and easy to use machines

"Give the customer the most innovative and technological product on the market"

3. Focus/ Niche

4. Economic Engine

Figure 4.6: The strategy triangle – Dyson

To make sure Dyson has the recruits it needs to continue its engineering excellence, it started the Dyson Institute of Engineering and Technology in 2006, partnering with the University of Warwick. Students work in the company for three days a week and receive a salary.

Finally, let's take an example of a company that delivers customer intimacy extraordinarily well: Home Depot (Figure 4.7). Customer intimacy is equally at home in the corner shop or the local deli. Remember the products must be up to a minimum standard and so must your operational efficiency, but where customer intimacy really hits home is delivering what each customer needs (personalization).

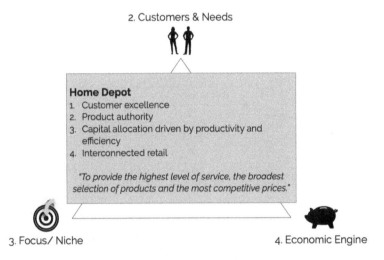

Figure 4.7: The strategy triangle – Home Depot

Home Depot, founded in 1978, is now the world's largest home improvement retailer. Its staff spend whatever time is necessary with a customer to find out what they need to solve their DIY problem, so their targets will not be about how many customers they see in a day, but rather about customer satisfaction. Customers who want a lower price will not go to a Home Depot store, as they must have a correspondingly higher price than their competition in order to invest money in the right staff, with the right level of customer service training.

So, what is your strategy? Where do you get your competitive advantage from? Use the strategy model in Figure 4.8 to figure out what your strategy should be, and it will give you the fourth critical area of your decision filters.

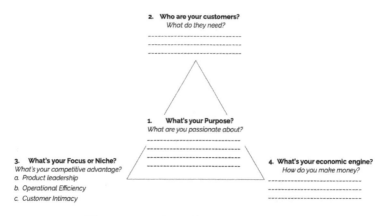

Figure 4.8: Creating your strategy

With your strategy in place, it will be easy to have those annual leadership meeting discussions on where to focus the following year and how much to invest and where. For example, a product-led strategy must have investments in R&D and must put highly skilled people in that area. A customer intimacy strategy will invest in the training and development of its front-line people and processes and systems that make it easier for the customer. Finally, an operational efficiency strategy will focus on highly efficient systems and processes, automation and high utilization of people, transport and machines. When you align your business behind your strategy, the Key Performance Indicators (KPIs) that you need (see Chapter 11 for a full explanation of how to set KPIs) will be obvious to you.

The tools of strategy

A chapter on strategy would not be complete without an introduction to the main tools that organizations use to help their strategic thinking. The reason for using these tools is that they help you to reach the right strategic decisions. There are numerous tools out there, some more useful than others. I will share those I feel are the most useful for organizations, and in particular senior leadership teams, to use on a regular basis to influence their strategic priorities.

The SWOT analysis

The SWOT analysis tool[4] has been a mainstay of strategic planning since the 1960s. It is credited to Albert Humphrey, who developed the approach at the Stamford Research Institute. The approach can be used for a whole organization, or equally well for individual departments, divisions or teams within it.

The acronym SWOT stands for Strengths, Weaknesses (these are both internal to the organization), Opportunities

---

[4] SWOT is accredited to Albert Humphrey of the Stamford Research Institute in the 1960s.

and Threats (both are external to the organization). The SWOT analysis allows an organization to put a stake in the ground and create real clarity and alignment about how the organization is doing today. It is best run as a team exercise and carried out quarterly. I always use a SWOT when working with a senior leadership team (SLT) to create the context for its annual planning sessions. The key is to build on your strengths and opportunities and address your weaknesses and threats.

Some preparation is required before using the SWOT tool with a team, especially for the external two areas. I will always ask members of the team to carry out research about the external opportunities and threats before the meeting.

The PESTLE analysis

The PESTLE (or PEST) analysis tool[5] is a deeper dive into the external environment and requires a more detailed amount of research before sharing with the team and gaining more input from them. It is often used to assess the market that a company wishes to launch a new product in and can equally be used as a more extensive analysis of the external environment in conjunction with a SWOT analysis.

- *Political.* These factors look at how a government is influencing or may influence the economy – for example, they may impose new taxes or trade tariffs.

---

[5] Francis Aguilar, *Scanning the Business Environment*, 1967, originally known as ETPS.

- *Economic.* These factors address what the economic performance looks like and how this may affect the business – for example, inflation, interest rates, foreign exchange rates, economic forecasts.
- *Social.* These factors scrutinize the social environment in the country or region. They are factors that may influence your business, such as cultural trends, demographics and buying trends.
- *Technological.* This area is mainly about innovations that may affect the business, such as automation, R&D and consumer responses to new technologies.
- *Legal.* The laws that may affect your business operations – for example, consumer laws, health and safety standards, employment laws.
- *Environmental.* This area is particularly relevant to businesses operating in the tourism, farming and agriculture industries. It considers factors such as climate and changing weather patterns, geographic location and carbon offsets.

The Boston Matrix

The Boston Matrix[6] was developed by the Boston Consulting Group (BCG) back in 1968. It was originally designed to help companies assess their product line or portfolio. It looks at market growth on one axis and relative market share on the other.

---

[6] Boston Consulting Group, *Boston Matrix*, 1968.

When putting your products, services or experiences on the matrix, you can add another dimension, which is the size of the circle. This can show the revenue to the company (bigger circle = more revenue) or any other relevant measure you want to review, such as profit or percentage of market share.

- *Stars.* In the top left box of the matrix are stars. Any of your products, services or experiences in this box have rapid growth and a dominant market share. They require investment to hold their position in the market and will generate a lot of income for the business.
- *Cash cows.* In the bottom left box, you have cash cows. Products, services or experiences in this quadrant require less investment as there are fewer competitive pressures. This is usually a low-growth market where the product dominates, generating significant revenue for the business.
- *Dogs.* The bottom right box has dogs. These products, services or experiences are likely to be making very little profit or a loss. They always have a weak market share in a low-growth market. The action for a dog is usually to withdraw it.
- *Question marks.* The top right box contains question marks. These are tricky to assess. The market is a growing one, but the products, services or experiences are not doing well. It could be because they are new to the market, in which case they may need more investment.

Ideally, organizations want to have a good mixture of cash cows and stars, and it is the dogs and question marks that must be considered carefully.

Ansoff Matrix

The Ansoff Matrix[7] is my favourite strategic analysis tool. It is used to weigh up the risks of expansion. Again, there are four quadrants and two axes. The traditional model shows markets on one axis and your products and services on the other. Each axis then shows 'existing' in the first box and 'new' in the second. You can plot all your existing products, services and experiences on the four squares of the grid and see for yourself where they sit. You can then decide whether you want to sell your existing products in new markets (market development) or develop totally new products and sell them into either existing markets or (the most risky) into new markets.

You can change the market axis to customers or consumers. The matrix can then be used to see what products and services you can cross-sell into existing customers, existing products and services to new customers (prospects), or new products and services into new customers. Like the Boston Matrix, you can draw a circle and use the size to demonstrate the revenue (or profit, etc.) of the product or service.

---

[7] Igor Ansoff, 'Strategies for Diversification', *Harvard Business Review*, September–October 1957.

Scenario planning (and forecasting)

Scenario planning[8] does just what it says on the tin. It is often used in a changing marketplace or when a business faces significant challenges, such as the 2020 Coronavirus pandemic. It allows a business to assess a range of outcomes before choosing what course of action to take. Here are the key steps to follow:

- Identify the critical challenges facing your business. These will have come out of your SWOT or PESTLE analysis.
- Assess what the possible outcomes might be for each of these – for example, during the pandemic a critical unknown was how long the 'lockdown' would continue for. Answer A – three months and answer B – nine months.
- Now consider what the permutations are of the different possible outcomes – each permutation is then one scenario.
- What would the impact be on the organization of each of the scenarios? In the above example, you would work out the impact of the scenarios of a lockdown lasting both three months and nine months.
- Identify the early warning signs. These will tell you the probability of each of the scenarios playing out.
- Identify what you can do (if anything) to influence the outcomes of the different scenarios. In our example, are you able to lobby the Institute of Directors, the

---

[8] Scenario planning is attributed to Herman Kahn in the 1950s.

Chamber of Commerce or your local government representatives?

- Evaluate the strategic choices you can take in your business against the scenarios. Be clear on their impact. Now you are in a good position to take strategic decisions, while monitoring the external environment for signs of how the scenarios are playing out.

In line with scenario planning, you will be carrying out scenario forecasting. One mistake that can be made here is to jump straight to the forecasting before you have thoroughly evaluated the scenarios.

Porter's five forces

It wouldn't be right to list the main tools of strategy and not include any by the man many consider the 'Godfather of strategy', Michael Porter (in addition to his three generic strategies mentioned at the start of the chapter). His book, *Competitive Advantage*, has had pride of place on my bookshelf ever since I completed my MBA in the early 1990s! Porter's work is deep and can be difficult to get your head around, but it is worth persevering. I'd also recommend Joan Magretta's *Understanding Michael Porter* as a great way to understand Porter's work.[9] Fundamentally, Porter's five forces framework[10] centres on how to make profits in your industry. It allows you to gain insight into your industry's performance

---

[9] Joan Magretta, *Understanding Michael Porter*, 2011.

[10] Michael Porter, *Competitive Strategy: Techniques for Analysing Industries and Competitors*, 1998.

and your own. As Porter says, the real point of competition is not 'to be the best' or beat your competition: it's to earn profits.

Everyone is in competition for profits in your industry. If your suppliers are powerful and make more profits, that impacts yours. If your customers are all powerful, they will demand more and pay less, and that impacts your profits. The five forces framework assesses the competition you face, and asks you to understand your industry's average prices and costs – and therefore the average profitability you are trying to beat. The insights presented from using Porter's five forces will lead to better decision-making about where and how to compete.

Set your strategy

Questions for you and your leadership team

1. Do you have a clear strategy that shows how you create your competitive advantage?
2. Does your leadership team understand the strategy of your competitors?
3. Does your leadership team understand and build plans (strategic priorities) on the platform that your strategy gives you?
4. Does everyone in your business understand your strategy?
5. Do you use your strategy to make critical decisions in your business?

Summary of Part 1

Part 1 of *The Leadership Map* will set your business up for success. Finding your purpose will connect you, your leadership team and all your people with the reason for your existence. With a well thought-through purpose, you don't need to sell any more: your sales people will have the belief that people need what you have because in some way it makes their lives better – just as Disney believes it is creating happiness, or TeamSport Indoor Go Karting believes it is creating exciting experiences and Southwest Airlines believes it is connecting people to what is important in their lives.

With a descriptive vision in place, you'll create excitement about the future and provide the challenge your people need to stretch themselves. Your vision will provide real guidance when crafting your annual strategic priorities and allow everyone in your business, wherever they sit, to connect their job to it. When John F. Kennedy was visiting NASA in 1961, he asked a janitor who was cleaning the floor what he did at NASA and he replied, 'I'm helping to put a man on the moon.' That's the power of an inspiring vision.

When your values are clear, you'll know who to recruit, who to promote and who to ask to leave your business because they don't fit. You'll be able to praise people based on behaviours linked to your values, which will reinforce them. And when a crisis comes along, you'll be able to use your values to help you make the right decisions.

Finally, a clear strategy shows everyone how you are different and where your sustainable competitive advantage lies. It helps you to decide what to do and where to invest your hard-earned cash.

Thinking deeply about your business is important. Those in your leadership team will get huge value, which they will apply in the ways they go about their day-to-day work, through the process of thinking through why you exist as a business, where you want to be in three years' time, how you want to behave and how you create sustainable competitive advantage. Don't underestimate the process. Therefore, these four strategic decision filters must be given time to create and the whole leadership team must be involved.

In Part 2 we will turn to people and teams. As a leader, most of your time will be spent on people issues: how to get them motivated, engaged, happy, working in highly effective teams, coming up with great ideas and facing the inevitable challenges you will face with grit and resilience.

PART 2
People and teams

Chapter 5

Challenge the status quo

Failure is not the opposite of success, it's part of success.
– Ariana Huffington

Introduction

When I run the People and Teams workshop as part of my Leadership Map programme, challenging the status quo always provokes a lot of interest. Leaders know intuitively that this is important, but are not sure quite why, or how to do it. In his book *Leaders Eat Last*,[1] Simon Sinek summed it up well when he said that leaders make it safe enough to take risks. The key here, as we see again and again, is that employees always take their lead from the top team and especially the CEO. The logic is simple: if you want to grow and develop people and cultivate new ideas, you must take risks, you must step outside your comfort zone, you must try new things. However, no one in your business is going to do this unless you do it. The key to growth is to try, fail and learn. Like many parts of The Leadership Map, this is a key ingredient of culture. I couldn't agree more with the

---

[1] Simon Sinek, *Leaders Eat Last: Why Some Teams Pull Together and Others Don't*, 2014.

comment from Ariana Huffington, the owner of *The Huffington Post*, quoted at the start of this chapter.

Great organizational cultures, like Toyota (mentioned in Chapter 3), have 'challenge' at their centre: people set really high standards and challenge themselves to reach them, they challenge other people and hold them to account when they don't show determination to stretch themselves, they challenge the small things to get marginal gains and they challenge the big things to get sweeping change. This element of culture keeps everyone engaged and energized, and looking for improvements consistently, everywhere.

The comfort and stretch zones

There are several areas to discuss in this chapter. First, if we want to get people to step outside of their comfort zone, how do we make this happen? One word: safety. Leaders must demonstrate that when people don't get it right, they are supported and coached, not criticized. Failure must be okay. It must be talked about. It must be put into context. What is failure anyway? Failure to one person may be coming second in a race by 0.2 of a second and to another person it may be not qualifying for the race at all. The first would be a success to many of us! When people set extraordinarily high standards, failure becomes a matter of degrees. What also puts failure into context is focusing on what you can control, not what you can't control. In a race, you can't control how fit or fast the opposition may be, the weather, the track you are running on or the number of people who show up to watch. What you *can* control is the amount of training you put in, the knowledge you gained through understanding more about your opponents and how they run, the gear you wear and the nutrition and hydration you take on board. When you set high standards and you prepare meticulously, and then you deliver the best you can, that's all you can do.

At work it is no different. You want to win a client contract. There are several things you can control: how much you know about the client's business, how well you build a relationship with them before the pitch, how well you know their strategy and their requirements and what they are prepared to pay. How well do you understand the competition who might be pitching against you? How will you differentiate your pitch? When you put everything into it, you have far more chance of success and no one should criticize you for not winning if the competition had a better solution. Following the pitch and the result, it is important to debrief and learn what went well and what could have been done even better. I will share a model to support this thinking later in the chapter.

So, let's suppose we now feel that our leaders and our peers have got our back (we have that feeling of safety). If we don't win the pitch or recruit the rising star we want or produce the breakthrough product within the timeframe, we know we'll be okay. We won't be fired, there won't be personal digs, there won't be political games, but there will quite rightly be challenge. However, we're happy with that because that is what high-performing teams and cultures have. So, stage one is complete: we feel comfortable taking on a challenge and putting ourselves in the spotlight. But feeling supported to do it and doing it are two different things.

Let's look at the model in Figure 5.1. The status quo is staying in our comfort zone. It's where nothing can go wrong, it's what we've done many times before to a certain standard and we are comfortable with it.

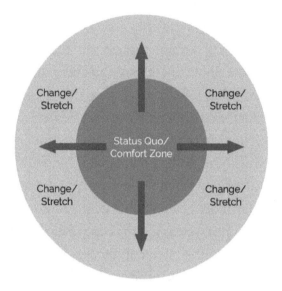

Figure 5.1: The change–stretch model

The problem with the status quo is that the longer we stay there, the harder it is to break out of it. The circle gets bigger and the prospect of stepping into change and stretch can be daunting. Unfortunately, when people stay in their comfort zone at work it becomes obvious and we say things like, 'She doesn't like change' or, 'Don't give the job to him, he just won't be up to it!' It's not their fault: the problem is that no one has made them feel safe and coached them into stretch and change. Stay too long in the status quo and you will become bored and stale, you increasingly believe that it is all you can do. You can then reinforce the fact that challenge, stretch and change are just not for you.

Encouraging people out of their comfort zone requires skill and patience. To do anything in life, there has to be a purpose, a goal, a reason. It is unlikely to be the same for every person in your business. Find out their motivation. There are two things you must explore with them: what are their fears and what are their dreams? Let's start with fears and then move onto dreams. Frank Dick was the strategic planning consultant for the England Rugby Football Union in 2019 and he has also been high performance director for South African Sports Confederation and Olympic Committee (SASCOC) and director of coaching at British Athletics. In short, he has huge experience of working with elite athletes and teams who want to win. What he saw regularly in the people with whom he worked was what he called four fatal fears:

1. the fear of getting it wrong
2. the fear of losing
3. the fear of rejection
4. the fear of criticism.

As a leader, you must find out what people are afraid of and reassure them that these fears are normal, and that you and their team will support them through their challenges. If these fears become too strong in people, they will simply never move forward with conviction towards their dreams and goals.

Next, what are their dreams? What do they want to be and do in three to five years' time? What would a perfect job look like for them? What really excites them? These are all great leadership coaching questions, which can help people to focus on the future. When that reason becomes compelling, and they feel reassured you'll support them, there is reason to step into stretch and change. The business and the team can also provide this. As I discussed in Chapter 1, a business purpose can be so inspiring that people will want to push themselves to do their part to achieve it. The challenge and support of a team can also be so strong that people don't want to let their colleagues down.

The real magic starts to happen when someone willingly steps into their stretch zone, has a compelling reason to go there, prepares incredibly well and knocks it out of the park! It's a buzz, the challenge energizes them, the praise from their colleagues is amazing, they want to do it again – it's now become a drug! The stretch zone can then become the norm. It gets bigger. They look for the next goal, the next big challenge, the next thing to learn; they realize how much there is to learn, the excitement mounts, they become unstoppable. That's what great leaders do. They help to create teams around them with a growth mindset, who are looking for that next challenge.

This, of course, isn't just good for business. The business will benefit enormously, the results will improve and success will build on success. The key to this, though, is to focus on the individual. When an individual grows, they become energized, they look for goals without prompting – in fact, you'll have to keep stretching them or they are likely to leave you and find an organization where they can flourish so their life becomes fulfilled.

PDCA

Let's now examine a model known as PDCA, which stands for Plan, Do, Check and Act. This will help us to ensure that we learn and grow from both our successes and our failures when we challenge the status quo. PDCA is a great tool at both an organizational and a personal level. It has had various iterations and versions over the years.

The P stands for Plan. I will talk separately in detail about the business planning process in Chapter 10. Organizations, departments, teams and individuals need a plan – what they intend to do over a given period of time. The plan will have actions associated with it and targets for each of the actions. It should also have accountabilities associated with each of the actions, as they apply to people, within your plan. However, plans almost never go exactly as they are intended to! To quote Mike Tyson,[2] 'Everyone has a plan until they get punched in the mouth.' Plans change because things happen that you couldn't foresee. You will not go through a year in a business and achieve everything you set out to achieve. Some plans are exceeded, in some you will under-perform and with others you just stop because something didn't work. You must know what to continue, what to change and what to stop.

The D stands for Do. This is when you monitor, adjust and communicate what happened over the course of the last month (for strategic plans) and the last week (for tactical plans). When you don't achieve a target over a given time

---

[2] Former professional boxer and undisputed world heavyweight champion between 1987 and 1990.

against forecast, then you need to adjust things rather than merely hope they will improve. It could mean putting more people in the team, providing more money, partnering with another business, adjusting the target or stopping the activity altogether. When you've decided what adjustment to make, you need to communicate them to the business. These first two steps are done by most organizations in some shape or form, some brilliantly and some less so.

Steps three and four are often not done well or not done at all. The third step is C for Check. You now need to check what went well and what went wrong. These sessions are best run with all the stakeholders involved. Start with what went well. It is so important to reinforce, celebrate and repeat the things you do well in business, so talk about them and agree what they are. Next, look at what went wrong. This vital step is about process, not people. It is not about personal attacks. If the product didn't work and everyone did their job, then the process of creating the product needs to be examined.

The final step is A for Act. Now you've examined what went well and what didn't go well, you must make sure that the relevant processes and systems are altered or new ones created so that the lessons learned are embedded in the business. This process is also known as open loop thinking: we do something, we learn what went well and what didn't go so well, we embed our learning in the business with new or adjusted processes and systems. Then the next person or team to do the same thing adopts the new approach. Closed loop thinking is exactly the opposite: things that happen in a room stay in a room and no one learns or changes.

5 Whys

The 5 Whys analysis tool[3] is the simplest of tools, but very effective nonetheless. When we spot a point of tension or a problem in our business that we need to challenge, the 5 Whys will help us to diagnose the real issue. The danger is that we don't look deeply enough for the root cause of the problem. We are often in too much of a rush to solve the problem so we spend too little or no time at all, accepting the first idea that emerges and putting a sticking plaster on it. The danger is that we then treat the symptom and not the root cause, so the problem happens again and again until we find the real issue. In Toyota, where the 5 Whys is used extensively, there is a step before 5 Whys, which is to make sure you know what the real problem is. This step is all about observation. We need to examine what is going on and compare it with the standard. One of Toyota's values discussed in Chapter 3 is *Genchi Genbutsu* (get a deep understanding of the situation). Stop too early and you have the wrong diagnosis of the problem. By asking enough 'Whys' (and it can be more than five) we can ensure that we get to the root cause and then address it directly. Just think about how much more efficient an organization becomes when you always go to the root cause before implementing solutions!

How our people react to change

One of the key tasks of leaders is to understand how individuals are reacting to the changes around them. In both the big

---

[3] The 5 Whys technique was developed by Sakichi Toyoda (1867–1930).

changes and the small changes, our people react at different speeds and in different ways. The Kubler-Ross[4] change curve (or grief cycle as it was originally known), which was developed in 1969 by the Swiss psychiatrist, shows the reaction of terminally ill patients when they find out they are dying. The model has been adapted many times over the years and is still a very useful model today. A CEO I worked with carried a laminated version around in his pocket and asked his staff, when relating to a change with which they were being faced, where they saw themselves on the curve. It is revealing to discuss where we are and where others see us. That way, we can explore how to move on to the next stage. It is also vital to understand the model ahead of changes you might be bringing in, in order to predict what your people are likely to go through and therefore to create a communications and engagement plan accordingly.

There are several things to be aware of when using this model. First, people go through change at different speeds, not everyone goes through every step, the steps are not always linear and people can go forward and then backwards through the steps. The important thing as a leader is to know where your people are, accept that and help them to move through the stages.

One problem leaders suffer from when taking people through change is to try to short-cut the learning they went through, and assume that by telling people their conclusions, people will buy in, engage and accept the change. This is not the case. When the status quo has been challenged and a new change has been accepted by a senior team (often the

---

[4] Elisabeth Kubler-Ross, *On Death and Dying*, 1969.

leadership team), they need to follow a sequence of steps to take people on the journey and get them through the change curve. This sequence has been documented over the years through different models; the two I have found most helpful are Kotter's eight steps[5] and Celemi's learning spiral[6] and one without the other will miss key steps. The model I show below integrates these approaches and shows them as a flywheel. The reason for the flywheel is that if one of these steps is missed out or badly implemented, the whole flywheel (and change programme) will stall.

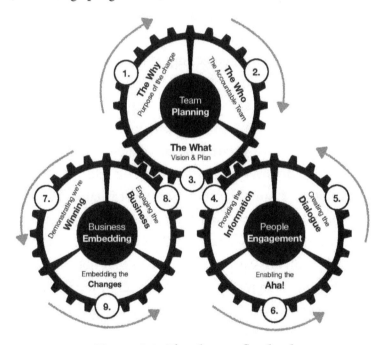

Figure 5.2: The change flywheel

---

[5] John Kotter, *Leading Change*, 1996.
[6] Klas Mellander, *The Power of Learning: Fostering Employee Growth*, 1993.

The first stage is team planning. The purpose of the whole programme must be clearly articulated, as this will be repeated constantly through the programme. The who is the accountable team – the people who will drive the whole programme through the business. They should not just be a sub-set of the leadership team; rather, the team should be representative of the organization and include natural influencers and local leaders, who will become change agents across the business. The final step in stage one is the vision and plan. There must be a clear vision of what the business will look like when the change has been implemented and what the plan is to get there.

The second stage is people engagement. Step four will be to recreate the story line of 'the why'. It is not enough to show people the outcome and the vision; they must understand the rationale if they are to really buy into the programme. In step five we must create a proper dialogue that engages our people in discovery and understanding – this is not just a presentation. Communication is not just what is said, it is what I hear, interpret and conclude. These dialogues must be carefully created and facilitated by the leaders of the business (external facilitators can be useful here, as they not only bring in their expertise in facilitation but also allow the leaders to own the programme and take part in it). If steps five and six have been well created and facilitated, people will have the necessary 'aha' moments and many will move to acceptance in the change curve.

The third stage is all about embedding the changes in the organization. It starts with step seven, sharing early wins so that people see that change is working. These are the wins that have been planned back in step three. Step eight is all about engaging everyone in the business to see what they need to do in their part of the business to make the change stick. Finally, step nine is where the changes need to be embedded in systems and processes across the business – either by changing existing ones or creating new ones.

Challenging the status quo is vital for a business: it keeps a business alive and full of energy, it fully engages its people allowing them to achieve their full potential and it creates a constantly changing and growing organism to flourish and grow.

Challenge the status quo

Questions for you and your leadership team

1. Does your culture readily encourage challenge and accept challenge?
2. Do you set stretch goals for yourself and others around you and support others to achieve them?
3. Do you operate an open loop culture in your business where feedback (both positive and negative) sessions are the norm and conducted regularly?
4. Do you and your leadership team understand how people react to change and know how to respond?
5. Do you have processes like the change flywheel and PDCA to help you manage change in your business?

Chapter 6

Develop your dream team

Vulnerability is having the courage to show up.

– Brené Brown

Introduction

I read a lot of books. You're reading this, so maybe you do too. There is a high correlation between reading lots of books and creating great teams – strange, huh? It's called intellectual humility. People who have high levels of intellectual humility are open to new ideas and to people who are different from them. When you are open to new ideas, you listen and you are intellectually flexible. This allows debate on the issue (not the person), as Lawrence Dallaglio explained from his time with the England Rugby team, at a conference I attended in 2019. Debate needs to create tension so that you get to the real issue, not vague artificial harmony that tackles the symptoms. But before we can look in more depth at how groups really tackle the tough issues, we must create trust, or what Patrick Lencioni calls vulnerability-based trust,[1] along with an environment that feels safe enough to open up.

---

[1] Patrick Lencioni, *The Five Dysfunctions of a Team*, 2002.

Go hard on the issue and soft on the person.
– Lawrence Dallaglio OBE, former England Rugby
Union Captain

In May 2012, I arrived in San Diego to complete a week's intensive training to become a Vistage Group Chairman. A Vistage Group Chairman's role is a strange and wonderful one; it's a combination of leader, facilitator, salesman, marketer, coach and mentor. The week-long programme challenged everyone to open up, challenge themselves, step outside their comfort zone and expose themselves emotionally. Not everyone made it through the week. If you are going to challenge, support and help CEOs to grow themselves and their business, then you must be on that journey yourself.

On the first morning, we were given 20 minutes to write a poem and be ready to stand up and read it to the rest of the 24 participants. The poem is called the I AM poem. It's about who you are, where you grew up, your challenges as a child, the music you liked, where you went to school, the friends you have, the values by which you live and much more. I was well outside my comfort zone! I wrote something, delivered it with a trembling voice and sat down to applause. Many of the group couldn't finish and there were others who broke down completely. Was this completely necessary? It was a revelation and the effect on everyone in the group was huge. Brené Brown's[2] books are central to this area, as she also believes vulnerability is one of our greatest assets. She describes it as follows:

---

[2] Brené Brown, *Daring Greatly: How the Courage to be Vulnerable Transforms the Way We Live, Love, Parent and Lead*, 2012.

Vulnerability is not winning or losing; it's having the courage to show up and be seen when we have no control over the outcome. Vulnerability is not weakness; it's our greatest measure of courage.

– Brené Brown

What happened that morning, facilitated skilfully by two future colleagues of mine, changed the room and laid the foundations for the week ahead. We suddenly became closer. We had shared things that some people had never before shared with virtual strangers. The barriers had been broken down and we had a deeper understanding of those around us. You cannot theorize about this; you must experience it. When I facilitate high-performing team-building programmes, I set people various exercises to do and I always go first. As a leader, that is one of the biggest lessons you must learn early on: if you don't show vulnerability, then no one else will either.

I changed that day, and during that week. I had been brought up in a family where children were seen but not heard. At the age of nine I went to boarding school in England, while my parents headed off to Pakistan, where my Dad worked at the British High Commission in Islamabad. You didn't show vulnerability at boarding school – no one did. Vulnerability was exploited and picked on. It was seen as weakness, whereas the reality is that it is a strength. As Brené Brown says, we often see vulnerability as a strength in others, but as a weakness in ourselves.

I shared my I AM poem with my family. I cried, my wife choked up and we hugged. It brought us even closer together. I realized how powerful it was to help executives to show their own vulnerability. This is for the very powerful reason that if you want your team to show up and put their real issues and challenges on the table, then as a leader you have to show that you don't have all the answers too and that starts with showing vulnerability. Leaders are role models and your teams copy how you act, not what you say.

The team excellence model

Our culture craves excellence, yet it is committed to creating an illusion that we can all have it with relative ease. Often we view critical feedback and conflict as damaging and to be avoided. Some CEOs can even be heard to say, 'I leave that to other people, it's not my thing.' The problem is that it goes hand in hand with being an effective leader. It's essential, and to avoid tough conversations is to erode your credibility as a leader. Tough conversations, focused on the issue not the person, must be the norm and the more you have them the less of a problem they become.

We must aspire to create team excellence, and we must not confuse it with being merely good, otherwise there is nowhere to go. To be excellent is a mindset more than an outcome; it requires a never-ending quest to learn and grow. Stanford professor Carol Dweck, in her book *Mindset*,[3] describes people with a growth mindset as 'those who believe that their success depends on time and effort. People with a growth mindset feel their skills and intelligence can be improved with effort and persistence.'

---

[3] Carol Dweck, *Mindset: The New Psychology of Success*, 2007.

We must be careful as leaders not to confuse short periods of excellence with *being* excellent. For example, we could deliver an excellent pitch or write an excellent report, and these might be highlights of a merely average week. When building a high-performing team, with excellence at its core, we must start in two places. The first is to understand where the team is now – how good is it really? This is arrived at from the second point, which is to have a common understanding of where the bar is being set and what excellence really looks like. Now we can see there is a gap, we can start to map out actions to bridge it. The starting point is real honesty and vulnerability between each member of the team. As I said in the Introduction to this book, leadership is tough, so if vulnerability, honesty and tough conversations are not your thing, then maybe you need to review why you want to be a leader. Being open and vulnerable seems risky, but it's the only route to excellence and, like ambiguity, leaders must learn to live with it.

So let's look at the six steps to creating team excellence (Figure 6.1).

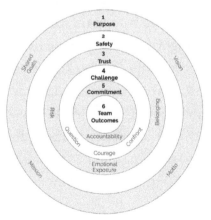

Figure 6.1: The team excellence model

Purpose

A team needs a reason to be together and it is important to state that up front and openly when a team is formed and when new members join. It is also useful to revisit this regularly to reinforce the primary purpose of the team being together, and perhaps what some of the immediate, shorter term reasons are for its existence. For example, the overriding purpose for the senior leadership team to exist will be to set the strategy and strategic priorities for the business, and the short-term goal may be a subset of that: to grow the profits of the business to a level that allows more investment back in the business. With this clearly articulated, and the leadership team aligned, you will have created a reason to put the important topics on the table and discuss them.

But purpose is just one of the things a team needs, and it is where a team (and an organization – see Chapter 1) must start. Following closely on the heels of a purpose, a team must have a vision that describes where the team wants to go and what it wants to be. This matters in elite sport as well as business. When Clive Woodward took over as head coach of the England Rugby team in 1997, he established a vision for the team to become the leading Rugby team in the world and win the Rugby World Cup.[4] His timeline was 1999, but unfortunately the boot of Jannie de Beer got the better of England that day at Twickenham stadium (the home ground of English Rugby) and England lost to South Africa 44–21. The vision didn't change: the desire grew and so did the team,

---

[4] Clive Woodward, *Winning: The Path to Rugby World Cup Glory*, 2004.

and in 2003 England became the top team in the world and beat the home team, Australia, in a thrilling final in Sydney.

The big difference between purpose and vision is that purpose has no timeline and vision does. A purpose often comes from the founder of the business, and the leadership team. The right purpose will inspire people to behave in a certain way and to seek excellence. Some organizations use different versions of a purpose to drive their people and teams onwards to ever-increasing levels of excellence. We can look at all kinds of jobs and see a purpose at the heart of the best ones. In Chapter 1 we looked at many great examples of organizational purposes, but it's not just businesses and sports teams that have them. The Special Forces may seem an odd place to go, but we can see that the UK SAS, the US Navy Seals and the French Foreign Legion all have mottos that guide their behaviours:

- *Navy Seals:* 'The only easy day was yesterday.' This shows the constant drive to improve and do a better job tomorrow.
- *SAS:* 'Who Dares Wins.' This shows that one of the key elements of the SAS is the boldness of its operations.
- *French Foreign Legion:* 'Honour and Fidelity.' The bar is set high, with all members holding each other in high respect and great esteem and completely faithful to the cause.

There are two other essential components of this first stage of team excellence: shared values and shared goals. I will not go into the importance of shared values in detail here, as Chapter 3 was devoted to this important area; however, a few key points are worth emphasizing. First, without shared values the team will simply fall apart. Strong leaders understand this and often are seen to make bold decisions to let someone who might be a good performer go rather than allow them to erode the shared values and behaviours of the group. Shared values must therefore be made explicit to members of the group and any new members, and they should be discussed in the context of making key decisions. The second area is shared goals. Shared goals are where you start and the achievement of them is where you finish. You must know what you are aiming at and you must remember to celebrate success when you achieve it. The shared goals must be created with team buy-in; they cannot be given to members of the team with the hope that they will be owned. My experience is that often, when teams are asked for their input on a goal, they create a harder one.

When a team knows why it exists (purpose), what it wants to be (vision), how it will behave (values) and what it wants to achieve (shared goals), it then has a foundation to develop towards excellence.

Safety

Jonathan McBride, MD of Blackrock, the world's largest asset manager and a former assistant to President Barack Obama, created a company that became one of *Fortune*'s Most Admired Companies, one of Human Rights Watch's Best Places to Work for LGBT Rights and one of LinkedIn's Top Companies 'Where the World Wants to Work'. He was absolutely clear that, 'You need people to care about each other. And how you get people to care is through emotional narrative.' When you have two people who don't get along, you can't just tell them to sort it out and work together. You need to get them to get to know each other, go out for lunch, not discuss work but rather find out about each other's background and values. In his experience, when this happens the people create a newfound respect for one another.

You need people to care about each other. And how you get people to care is through emotional narrative.
                              – Jonathan McBride, MD of Blackrock

Creating an environment of safety provides a platform for creating team excellence. Without a feeling of safety, why would team members open up? Why would they say what is on their minds? Safety is the feeling you get when you are surrounded by people who share the same values and purpose, and are committed to a common vision and set of goals. Safety must be demonstrated by the leader to show that when people are vulnerable, it's not just okay, it's good and must be encouraged. When people start an honest, tricky and sensitive conversation in the group that tackles the real issues, they should be applauded for doing so. Safety is made up of three key areas: belonging, caring and support. All three areas must be addressed when on-boarding people to a new team.

Team members must not only feel no danger from the boss, but also from every other team member. As Simon Sinek[5] says in his book *Leaders Eat Last*, 'We have to take the

---

[5] Simon Sinek, *Leaders Eat Last*, 2014.

danger away'. The danger in a business is all around us and can cause stress and anxiety (which increases cortisol and will erode our immune systems leading to illness and days off work). Dangers come from both external and internal sources. Externally, they come in the form of competition, from the economy, through losing customers, from the stock market, from new technologies and so on; internally, they stem from a fear of making a mistake, a self-limiting belief, fear of criticism and fear of losing.

Without safety, we spend time playing politics and protecting ourselves rather than opening up and discussing the important issues of the day. These essential ingredients of team excellence must be shown by leaders across the whole organization, not just in their team. These first two areas of the model offer practical things that leaders can do. When they do create a common purpose and sense of safety in the team, vulnerability, challenge, commitment and great outcomes will follow.

Trust

There are many ways of building trust in your team and you don't have to start straight away with a 'deep dive' like the I AM poem! In fact, I would go so far as to give a health warning. There are 'light' versions to get your group communicating before moving on to 'heavier and deeper' exercises.

One of the best ways to start in your team is a simple meeting sign-in. This can be run in so many ways by changing the questions and the categories; it's just down to your imagination.

Let's start with a regular weekly team meeting. You have six people in your team. You go around the table and ask people to provide a score out of 10 for 'personal' and 'business'. You can vary these by adding or changing them. I often use 'health and wellbeing' as a third category and leave the 'personal' category for family and relationships. Everyone must also be prepared to provide a short narrative of their past week, focusing only on the biggest challenges/issues/opportunities they have faced. A simple heading for this narrative can be 'your one big thing'. If you are the leader of the team, you must go first and your openness, vulnerability and emotional exposure will set the tone for everyone else. The scores in themselves open up great opportunities for discussion. What if one of your team scores a 6 for 'business' or 'personal'? This is likely to be a cry for help, which needs to be discussed either as a team or in a personal discussion following the meeting. The more you get people to open up and share their stories, the more others will care about them and feel able to challenge them about their issues.

The time to run deeper exercises is when you have off-site workshops, ideally with an overnight stay, when executives have time to unwind and really get to know their colleagues properly. Here are a number of exercises that you can run with your teams:

- *Two truths and one lie.* Get members of your team to prepare to share two things about them that are true and one that is a lie. This is a fun exercise as it forces people to make something up about their past. You learn how good your colleagues are at embellishing stories! The important thing is you also learn about two things that they are usually quite proud of. Perhaps they have done a sky dive, run a marathon, climbed a mountain or written a book. Whatever it is, tells you something about who they are, starts a behaviour of sharing and gives you something to talk about in the future.

- *My core values and where they came from.* Get your team to think deeply about what their personal core values are. These will have been developed from their upbringing, their family life and early schooling, and the people who have made a big impact on their lives.
- *Pivotal moments.* When members of your team have been faced with key challenges in their lives, how did they respond? What led to the decisions they took and what has been the impact?
- *80th birthday speech.* What do they want to achieve in their lives? This is a speech delivered by a partner, spouse, family member or friend in the future at their 80th birthday party. The speech outlines what they have achieved in their life, what values they have lived, what difference they have made to people and what they are still involved in. If 80 seems too far off for some, make it 50 or 60.
- *I AM poem* as outlined in the story above.

To get the most out of these exercises, make sure everyone presenting and listening is in the right frame of mind – off-site is best. I usually run these exercises over the course of a dinner when people are relaxed and perhaps enjoying a glass of their favourite drink. Several things are very important. First, they must be conducted in a private space where no one outside the team can hear. Second, as I've stressed many times before, the leader must go first to show that they are being open and transparent and how important they think the exercise is. Third, everyone should treat the person speaking and what they are saying with a great deal of respect: this is hard stuff, often people will choke up, so they need to be encouraged, not rescued, and applauded after their talk.

You can never stop working on trust in a team. It's the foundation of team excellence; the more trust you build, the deeper and more effective you will be in having those great conversations that focus on the key issues affecting your business. It's what gets you quickly to the challenging conversations, which is why it is so important.

Challenge

Great teams debrief. They debrief as soon as they can after the activity, whether it be a pitch to a client, the completion of a project or an internal presentation. They focus on what went well (WWW) and even better if (EBI). They are specific in discussing both – not using vague statements about how good they were, but by breaking down the key things that went really well, why they went well and how they will do them again and improve upon them even more in the future. Then they focus on where things didn't go so well, what happened, how and why it happened, what they need to do the next time, so that it will go well. To an outsider these conversations can seem hard, personal and at times negative, but they are what produces the big effective changes in people and processes that will move your business on to a new level. They rely on openness and vulnerability, and a growth mindset.

How often do 'corridor conversations' or coffee station conversations on important topics take place in your business? They should be banned, or at least always lead to the proper conversation that should take place in the meeting room with the right people attending at the right time.

I am an introvert. That means I process information in my brain *before* I say it, but it also means that working constantly in groups drains my battery and I need private time to recharge them. On the flip side, extroverts literally make it up as they go along! Extroverts speak and consider in parallel what they are going to say. They also get their energy from being in groups. See the problem? Knowing who we are and what that means has implications for us, and it has implications for groups and teams when they get together. For example, when you know you have an introvert in the group, don't spontaneously ask them a question and demand a quick answer. Rather, signpost the question and say you will come back to them for the answer or let them have questions in advance. Extroverts, on the other hand, love to give you an answer straight away, but it may not have been thought through so well!

I was attending a training course several years ago and the facilitator (who was brilliant) said he was an introvert and one of the ways he dealt with it was to make a pact with himself that if he thought something was important, he must say it at the time. He did not allow himself to have a good idea and leave the room with it still in his head! I have adopted this ever since and it's a great mantra to have for fellow introverts. It is critical for your team to understand the personality profiles of the members. You can use tools like DISC profiling or Merrick Rosenberg's Taking Flight with DISC[6] version. DISC is great, but people can forget it and Merrick has converted each of the letters into a bird, which is very memorable (see Chapter 12 for further details).

Challenge is vital in teams so that we discuss the real issues in depth and come up with answers. It is also vital because we need everyone in the team to debate the real issues: as Patrick Lencioni says, 'if we don't weigh in, we don't buy in'.[7] Teams operate on a spectrum of engagement. At one end of the engagement is inertia, apathy or artificial harmony. This is when the energy is low, the real issues aren't being put on the table, nothing is happening and we all want to get out of the meeting because we know it's a waste of time. At the other end of the spectrum we have destruction. Ideas are surfaced and shot down, personal digs are the norm and the atmosphere is toxic! We have almost certainly all been at some time in both types of meeting, probably more often the former than the latter.

The key is to create enough energy and tension around issues to keep it positive and productive without edging over into destruction. The more we move towards tension

---

[6] Merrick Rosenberg and Daniel Silvert, *Taking Flight! Master the DISC Styles to Transform Your Career, Your Relationships... Your Life*, 2011.

[7] Patrick Lencioni, *The Five Dysfunctions of a Team*, 2002.

and increased energy, the more possibilities we create for great outcomes in our meetings. This is where the role of the leader or leaders in the meeting must increase the tension and energy. You need to make sure you don't accept the 'nodding dogs' around the room when you discuss an idea. Look people in the eye and ask them what they are thinking. Get the discussion on the table, at the time!

Commitment

It is when, and only when, we get the proper, real, in-depth conversation about a topic happening that we achieve a proper resolution and outcome. We process the issue and we reach a conclusion. At this point, it is critical to get commitment to action(s). The commitment to doing something is likely to be there because of the deep conversations that have got to the heart of the problem (the root cause) and come up with a resolution – or at least a way forward. The person with the issue, who has likely weighed in the most in the discussion, will or should be the most committed to getting it done and move the thing forward, although at this point the whole team will be committed to seeing something happen.

Accountability must follow commitment, which is why I have put them together and not separated them out; a bit like success and failure, they are two sides of a journey towards a goal.

Once there is commitment in the room to seeing something happen and there is real energy behind this, you must nail down accountability. Accountability can only be owned by one person! You cannot and must not ever try to hold two people accountable in a team for the same thing – it's a road to disaster. Two or more people can work on the solution to deliver the outcome and more than one person can be responsible for aspects of the work, but at the top level, only one person can be accountable. Once you've established who is the most appropriate person in the team to be accountable, there is set of leadership coaching questions to go through. This approach is vital as you need the accountable person to own every part of the outcome and it must be run by the leader in the room. Here is the approach, and I'll use the example of a CEO talking to their marketing director, who is taking accountability:

CEO: So, tell us all (the team in the room) exactly what you have agreed to do?

Marketing director: I'll be writing a report, as discussed in this meeting, on the feasibility of launching our new product in the south of the country.

CEO: Which states will you include?

Marketing director: Initially just Alabama and Louisiana.

CEO: When will you have the report completed?

Marketing director: In three weeks' time.

CEO: Is that enough time? How about we say four weeks, in time for our next management meeting?

Marketing director: Okay, that's good.

CEO: Give us an indication of what to expect in terms of content.

Marketing director: Well, I guess similar to the last one I did six months ago on the West Coast – about 10 pages in PowerPoint.

CEO: That sounds great, can you circulate it to all of us one day before and I'll give you 30 minutes on the agenda to present and for discussion?

Marketing director: Yep, that sounds fine.

As you can see from this example, the CEO just asks questions in order to hold the marketing director accountable. Everyone in the team hears the answers and therefore the agreement is being shared with all team members, which is even more powerful.

Team outcomes

The reason for a team to exist is to create an outcome. Your business will ultimately be judged on results, and the buck stops with the leadership team and how it is led by the MD or CEO. Doing all the other things really well in the model will culminate in good outcomes and results. If you have a strong, well-articulated purpose and some shorter-term goals and targets, if you have created a safe environment where people feel supported and cared for, if you have encouraged and built trust in the team, if you have cultivated regular and challenging conversations, and if you end all meetings with a confirmation of your commitments and accountabilities, then you will get the results you deserve.

Teamship rules

One of the key 'rules' of an All Black is to embrace expectations, not only from your teammates, but also the country and most importantly yourself. The great All Black, Richie McCaw, the most capped player in the game with 148 caps, was sitting in a cafe with his uncle when he was a promising teenager. They were discussing Rugby and his uncle asked him what his ambitions were. The young Richie said he wanted to be an All Black. For most people, that would have been enough: to play for your national team – the most successful international Rugby team ever. His uncle turned to him and said, 'You don't want to be an All Black, you want to be a Great All Black!' McCaw was too embarrassed to write Great All Black down, so on the back of a napkin he wrote 'GAB'. That was enough: his sights were set. When he became an All Black, before every game the last thing he would ask himself was, 'What would a Great All Black do? How would a Great All Black behave?' The All Blacks don't want people to be All Blacks, they want people to be Great All Blacks.

One of the challenges in the teams we create and become part of is to have a clear understanding of where the bar is set. This is perhaps easier for a sports team, when you can have very clear and tangible targets, such as win every game and finish top of the league. In our work teams, it can some-times be harder to have this clarity. Perhaps the two most important words in leadership are 'clarity' and 'alignment'. How clear am I about what I need to do and are we, as a team, all aligned behind this?

As mentioned earlier, Clive Woodward took over the England Rugby team in 1997 and coached them through to a World Cup final, which they won in 2003. Along the way they had become the leading team in the world. When Woodward ran his first big meeting of the 'elite' squad, he realized he had quite a job on his hands. They strolled in late, many on their mobile phones, with a widely held view of 'What on earth am I doing in a meeting, when I could be training?' Woodward realized he needed to change things. He started by changing the question from 'What do we need to do to win with the resources at our disposal?' to 'If we are going to be the no. 1 team in the world and win the World Cup, then what would that team need to do, day in and day out to get there?'

Woodward was looking for a set of values, rules and stand-ards that would bind them together. He first heard the term 'followership' from a speaker called Humphrey Walters, who had sailed around the world. He didn't think it was about followership and so he wrote down the phrase 'teamship'. He believed that every single member of your team should have an input into key decisions. You need, as I've already said, a vision, purpose, strategy and values, and then a sense of one-ness. Using an external facilitator, Woodward got the team to write down the standards, rules and behaviours to which they would all sign up. These are the things the no. 1 team in the world would do! He put them into a small book, which was given to all new members of the team to also sign up to. They evolved over the years as the team did, but the essence would stay the same.

I've facilitated the creation of teamship rules for most of the leadership teams with which I've worked. I've had them printed out, laminated and turned into an upright table stand. They sit in the middle of the table at every meeting. It's another way of holding each other to account. You know as a leader when they are working well, when any member of the team quotes the teamship rules at another member and a positive discussion follows.

Picking and developing an outstanding team

Great leadership is not only about doing the 12 things in this book extremely well, it's also about accountability for the underlying things that really make the business sing. Picking and developing an outstanding senior leadership team is critical. The team leader will hold members accountable for developing and delivering on their plans, but who will hold them accountable to role model the values of the business and who will praise them for a job well done? If you ever catch yourself saying that there is no one who could possibly replace them in their roles in the business, then you have ultimately failed. Your senior leadership team must develop the next level down, as they are developing themselves.

For each of your subordinates, you must have a shared understanding of the 'grip' you need with them and the 'stretch' they need. Grip is how tightly you manage them in each part of their role and stretch is how far you need to push each of them. It is important to understand that this is a two-way model for each element of a person's job. Both parties, the line manager and the subordinate, must agree about where they are on the model for each element. The focus on the key stage of the model can then follow. I use a simple four-step process to work with people (Figure 6.2):

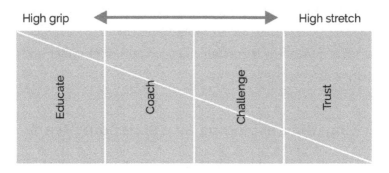

Figure 6.2: The grip–stretch model

1. *Educate.* How well do people understand what they need to do and what you expect of them? If this is unclear, they will either do the wrong thing or nothing at all.

2. *Coach.* Leadership has a lot to do with coaching. Your people need to be asked great questions and coached through the different elements in their role to deliver on their objectives.

3. *Challenge.* Once your people know what they are doing, you must challenge them to move up through the gears and stretch themselves so they will learn and grow, and deliver more. This is the stage from which we get our energy.

4. *Trust.* Finally, you can release the grip. Fantastic performers – and you will only have relatively few in any business – can be trusted to get on and deliver against your goals. They need little guidance. The big mistake many leaders make is that they jump to this fourth level very quickly, believing that the previous three levels are just micromanaging people.

Creating or being a part of a high-performing team is arguably the most important thing you can do as a leader. It's also the most challenging. It requires putting many of the other chapters into practice too: giving them a purpose, a vision and a common set of values, working with them to develop your strategy and strategic priorities, challenging them and having tough conversations when necessary, showing you care through motivating and engaging them and helping them to become more resilient. With a high-performing team, you can achieve the extraordinary.

Develop your dream team

Questions for you and your leadership team

1. How safe is your culture? Are people encouraged to stand up and try new ways of doing things?
2. Do you and your team demonstrate vulnerability and authenticity, because if you don't then why should others?

3. Do you 'mine for conflict' in your team meetings to get to the heart of the issues?
4. How accountable are people in your business?
5. Do you have a common set of 'rules' (e.g. teamship rules) that have been created by the team for the team?

Chapter 7

Engage the emotions

Happiness is a mindset for your journey, not the result of your destination.

– Shawn Achor

Introduction

A great culture sits at the centre of any great business. As leaders, we must encourage our people to really get involved and to see our business as more than just a way of making money or 'selling widgets'. In this chapter I will cover three essential ingredients of culture that are very different and interconnected: engagement, motivation and happiness. Culture comes from the Latin *cultus*, which means *care*. Great leaders care deeply about their people. The more I step into the murky and often misunderstood world of organizational culture, the more I realize how complex and important an area this is; these three areas are at the heart of it.

Engagement

Gallup research shows that when a manager ignores his or her people, the chances of those people being 'actively disengaged' are 40%.

Having a manager who ignores you is even more detrimental than having a manager who primarily focuses on your weaknesses!

– Tom Rath

Isn't that statistic awful! It basically says that people are more engaged in your organization even if they only get negative feedback all the time as opposed to *no* feedback. The key takeaway is that as leaders we must keep talking with our people about how they are doing.

So what is engagement? Gallup has given us a definition that it uses to assess levels of engagement in organizations around the world, with its staff survey tool Gallup Q12. You can see the research that went into this in Marcus Buckingham's book *First, Break All the Rules*.[1] Gallup has defined three levels of engagement in organizations:

1. *Engaged.* Loyal and committed to the organization. More productive, more likely to stay with their company.
2. *Not engaged.* May be productive but not committed to their company. They are more likely to miss workdays and more likely to leave.
3. *Actively disengaged.* Physically present but psychologically absent. They are unhappy with their work situation and insist on sharing that unhappiness with their colleagues.

---

[1] Marcus Buckingham and Curt Coffman, *First, Break All the Rules: What the World's Greatest Managers Do Differently*, 2005.

Gallup has worked with over 17 million employees in over 30 countries and every year it publishes its latest findings. You can use Gallup to run the survey in your business and it will benchmark your company against your industry, both in your country and globally. The 2017 findings are shocking across Western Europe, where employee engagement levels are exceptionally low. Regionally, just 10% of employees are engaged – involved in and enthusiastic about their work. By comparison, 33% of employees in the United States are engaged. This has a huge effect on productivity in our workplaces, so it is something that leaders must understand and address. As a comparison, Table 7.1 shows figures for the United Kingdom and the United States; for other countries, go to www.gallup.com and download the *State of the Global Workplace* report.

Table 7.1: Employee engagement levels

	Engaged	Not engaged	Actively disengaged
UK	11%	68%	21%
US	33%	53%	14%

My contention is that the most useful thing about the 12 questions in this survey is that they hold up a mirror to your leadership team to show you how well you are leading your business. You can also slice and dice the results against the different areas of your business to see high and low areas of engagement. In short, if you want engaged staff – loyal and committed to the organization, more productive, more likely to stay with their company – then you need to ask the right questions and act on them.

I often think of these three areas as giving us A, B and C players. A players are rare – they are, after all, only 11% of our workforce in 2017 in the United Kingdom (see Table 7.1). They are personally driven, they get to the top of their organizations and they often run their own businesses. They are hard to find and often even harder to keep. When you have them, you must set them stretching goals, challenge them and give them autonomy. B players will be the majority of the people in your business. They will come to work and will usually be productive, but if a better offer comes along they might well switch employers. So anything you can do to engage these B players, so that they really see the difference between your workplace and others, may retain more of them. You really shouldn't have too many C players, but in my experience you will always have some (and you and everyone else knows who they are) and they take up far too much time distracting you and others in the business. The problem with C players is that they insist on sharing their unhappiness with others, and therefore stand every chance of influencing others in a negative way – they can be poisonous!

For A and C players, you must have a plan. For the A players, what does their development look like? Are they being challenged with the right roles and projects? What do they really want to do in the business and can you give that to them? You may not be able to keep A players forever, so make the most of them and treat them well, because if they leave you then you want them to recommend others to your business. You must have tough conversations with your C players. They need to understand that they must either move upwards and become B or even A players, or 'we will set you free'. With C players, it usually starts with an attitude problem, which may move on to become a capability or focus problem with their work. Often an honest conversation can unlock the situation, but the longer it goes on, the worse it becomes. Keeping C players in the business for too long erodes the credibility of leaders. People will ask why they are still there. Your business does not owe people a living – they must earn it!

Motivation

In 1997, I was working as a senior consultant for Celemi, a learning design and communication company. Six months into the role, I sold and delivered a project to Sainsbury's, a large national grocery chain in the United Kingdom. I was driving back from a meeting in London with my boss and we stopped at a sports store to buy some cycling kit for him as he was an avid mountain biker. On leaving the store, he handed me a store bag and thanked me for delivering a great project. Inside was a golf shirt. I was a mad keen golfer then (I still am today) and it meant the world to me. The shirt was worth about £50 and I remember it to this day. Why? Because he knew what I loved to do outside of work, where my interests lay, and he rewarded me accordingly. So here is a simple thing that you can do if you lead people or work in a team:

1. Write down the names of those who you lead/interact with.
2. Against each name, write down what they love to do outside of work. It could be cooking, eating at nice restaurants, going to the movies, following a sports team.

3. If you don't know, then now is your chance to find out.

4. There are two things you can do with this information. This first is to deepen your relationship. You now know more about them and they might know more about you. This means you've developed more trust and when working together this will pay dividends as discussed in Chapter 6. Second, when they've performed well at work you can reward them according to what they love doing: a voucher at a great restaurant, tickets to the movies or to see their favourite sports team.

Now when you come to work on a Monday morning ask them what they have done, show a great interest in them and they will reward you with engagement. The bland 'How was your weekend?' followed by walking off with your coffee in the other direction will not cut it!

One thing to remember about feedback is that it needs to be timely (as soon as possible after they performed well) and specific (explaining exactly what they did). Both these things mean that the individual will know what to do the next time and is likely to repeat the good stuff. One of the great dangers of being a leader is that we feel we need to know the answer and to 'show leadership', and we feel we need to make sure everyone knows this! Research shows that quite the reverse is true. Don't be tempted when giving feedback to give too much advice, stick to the praise and don't sandwich around something they are not doing well because you feel you ought to. Remember, if you offer one piece of negative feedback, you will need to give five pieces of positive feedback to counter this and put the person in a positive state of mind.

Praise is infectious. In Shawn Achor's book, *Big Potential,*[2] he shows the effect that praise has, not only on the individual receiving it but also on the team around them. He shows that if you give four or more 'touchpoints' of praise over the course of a year, the praise they give to others doubles! New hires have an 80% retention rate, but with three or four praise touchpoints that increases to 94%! As we know from Gallup's Q12, mentioned earlier in this chapter, the frequency of the praise (and feedback in general) that we give is crucial. As leaders, we must be giving feedback to our staff every week. This is not an appraisal meeting. This is instant feedback on how they are doing.

Public praise is also important, as it releases a chemical called serotonin into the body. This gives people a feeling of pride, confidence, status and respect. Never forget the effect we can have on people when we praise them for a job well done.

Motivation comes in many forms. What we do know is that once you take money off the table (pay the going rate or just above for the job and the industry) then it isn't a motivator anymore. In fact, studies have shown that the reverse can be true. In Dan Pink's book *Drive*[3] and his TED Talk, he puts forward the case that we are motivated by three things:

[2] Shawn Achor, *Big Potential: How Transforming the Pursuit of Success Raises Our Achievement, Happiness, and Well-Being,* 2018.
[3] Dan Pink, *Drive: The Surprising Truth About What Motivates Us,* 2009.

mastery, autonomy and purpose. Let's look at these three areas in a bit more detail:

1. *Mastery.* Mastery is getting better at those things we really enjoy. For me it is reading, listening, watching and learning more about leadership. For example, I recently watched the Netflix series on Michael Jordan called *The Last Dance*. It is an amazing insight into arguably the best player ever to have graced the basketball court. This great series made me wonder how his coach, Phil Jackson, managed this amazing team, so I went on to read Jackson's autobiography, *Eleven Rings*,[4] which refers to the 11 championships he coached teams to win. Phil Jackson led the Chicago Bulls with a team of superstars (and egos), including Michael Jordan, Scottie Pippen and Dennis Rodman. He worked with his team to constantly develop their mastery. What he was great at was getting them to not only develop their individual mastery, but to work together as a team. Rodman was a phenomenal player who toughened up the Bulls, but he was a law unto himself. Rodman dated Madonna, went off to wrestle with Hulk Hogan before a game and famously went on a trip to Vegas during the 1997 NBA Finals against the Utah Jazz. Jackson's coaching style was that if Rodman turned up for the games and put in a performance, he could cope with his antics. Contrast that with Steve Hanson's eight-year reign coaching

---

[4] Phil Jackson, *Eleven Rings: The Soul of Success*, 2013.

the All Blacks (New Zealand) Rugby team with a win ratio of 89%! The constant growth mindset and developing the mastery of the players in the All Blacks is legendary, but he did it in a very different way from Jackson, showing that great leaders come in all sizes and shapes. There is no room for egos and lack of discipline in the All Blacks; at the end of a game it is the senior players who, after their debriefs, 'sweep the sheds'. They literally clear up the changeroom – it keeps them grounded. Within the New Zealand All Blacks, personal discipline and humility are high on their list of necessary qualities to be in the team. With both coaches and with all the extraordinary athletes that made up the teams they coached, mastery was at their centre. A mindset of learning and growing every member of the team, every day, to become a better version of themselves was a fundamental principle.

2. *Autonomy.* As Steve Jobs once said, 'It doesn't make sense to hire smart people and tell them what to do; we hire smart people so they can tell us what to do.' We know that isn't simple to do. With autonomy comes responsibility, so you cannot give autonomy to people who can't perform at the necessary level or who don't have the right character to go and ask for help if they need it. In Chapter 6 I talk about the grip–stretch model. This is a great model to use when figuring out when to give people full autonomy. As a leader, you must be sure that everyone in your team knows exactly what to do and what is expected of them, then they need to be coached to constantly improve their

performance before being challenged to stretch and grow themselves. In Chapter 9 I also talk about the intent-based leadership model as described by David Marquet in his book, *Turn the Ship Around*,[5] which is all about growing leaders by giving them accountability. Before accountability is given to a person, a leader can test their readiness through questioning: how well do they understand the situation, have they thought through the options, what do they recommend should be done, what do they intend to recommend? Only when you can be sure your people are at that stage should you give them autonomy.

3. *Purpose.* I've devoted a whole chapter to purpose in this book (see Chapter 1), as it is clear that without a 'why', our motivation will drop. Gallup describes purpose as a 'bold affirmation of its reason for being in business, it conveys what the organization stands for in historical, ethical, emotional, and practical terms'. You can be motivated by your organization's purpose or create your own – or both. When I work with individuals, I help them create their own personal purpose, and that will show them how congruent their purpose is with the purpose of the organization. It is therefore vital that you have a great organizational purpose and that everyone in your business really gets it. Here are some other great examples of purpose in different types of organizations:

---

[5] David Marquet, *Turn the Ship Around: The True Story of Turning Followers into Leaders*, 2012.

- IKEA: To create a better everyday life for the many people.
- Nordstrom: To give customers the most compelling shopping experience ever.
- TED: To spread ideas.
- WWF: To create a world where people and wildlife can thrive together.
- Kellogg food company: Nourishing families so they can flourish and thrive.

Happiness

The world of happiness has become a popular area to study. It's a combination of many things: pleasure, hope, faith, trust, optimism, ecstasy, calm, joy, flow, satisfaction, contentment, pride and serenity. Much of it is written and talked about under the heading of positive psychology. As the quote at the start of this chapter states, happiness is not something we can seek out and find. It does not come from buying a big house, a flash car or a new watch. These things tend to give us short-term joy, but not long-term, enduring happiness. Happiness is therefore something we create in our mind in the way we look at the world. Martin Seligman starts his book, *Authentic Happiness*,[6] with a story about the longevity of nuns in the School Sisters of Notre Dame in Milwaukee, USA. These 180 nuns enjoyed exactly the same lifestyle and ate the

---

[6] Martin Seligman, *Authentic Happiness: Using the New Positive Psychology to Realise Your Potential for Lasting Fulfilment*, 2004.

same things. They became the subject of a study of happiness and longevity. All the nuns were asked to write essays when they took their final vows before committing the rest of their lives to teaching young children. Some wrote positive, happy and uplifting essays and others, by contrast, 'had not even a whisper of positive emotion'. Analysis revealed that 90% of the most-cheerful quarter were alive at the age of 85, whereas only 34% of the least-cheerful quarter were. Seligman concluded that a happy nun is a long-lived nun.

It has often been said that happiness makes you smile and smiling makes you happy – but how true is that? Is there a fake smile? It turns out that there is. A genuine smile is when the corners of your mouth turn up and the skin around the corners of your eyes crinkles. It's called a Duchenne smile after the person who discovered it, Guillaume Duchenne. These muscles, it turns out, are extremely difficult to control voluntarily. A smile that doesn't have these features is therefore inauthentic. When trained psychologists look at photographs, they can tell an authentic (Duchenne) smile, from a non-authentic one. Two psychologists, Dacher Keltner and LeeAnne Harker, studied 141 class photos from the 1960 yearbook of Mills College, University of California at Berkeley. All but three of the women were smiling and only half of them were authentic Duchenne smilers. When the two psychologists inherited the study in the 1990s, they wondered whether they could predict how the women's lives had turned out. The results were astonishing. On average, the Duchenne women were more likely to marry and stay married, and to experience more personal wellbeing over the next 30 years.

The good news is that, like many things, happiness can be trained, and I will share a number of things we can do to build up our happiness muscles. Let's start by looking at some of the impact happiness has on people:

- Happy people take fewer days off sick. Oxytocin is released in the body when we feel love, trust and loyalty from great friendships. Oxytocin boosts our immune systems.
- Happy people are more receptive to learning. The dopamine that is released when we achieve goals and tasks activates our learning centres.
- Happy people are more confident people. When we are publicly recognized and respected, a shot of serotonin is released, giving us a feeling of pride and boosting our status and our confidence.
- Adults with a positive wellbeing are 47% more likely to consume fresh fruits and vegetables and are 33% more likely to be physically active.[7]
- Happier people are more satisfied with their jobs than unhappy people, but further than that, research suggests that more happiness causes more productivity and a higher income.

---

[7] Laura Sapranaviciute-Zabazlajeva, Dalia Luksiene, Dalia Virviciute, Martin Bobak and Abdonas Tamosiunas, 'Link between healthy lifestyle and psychological wellbeing in Lithuanian adults aged 45–72: A cross-sectional study', *BMJ*, 7(4), 2017, www.researchgate.net/publication/315776636_Link_between_healthy_lifestyle_and_psychological_well-being_in_Lithuanian_adults_aged_45-72_A_cross-sectional_study.

- Adults and children put into a good mood set higher goals, perform better and persist longer on a variety of tasks.

Now let's dispel some of the myths of happiness. The first myth is that the accumulation of material possessions and accomplishments makes you happy. Actually, it just makes your expectations rise and there is little evidence that it makes you happier. Seligman calls this 'the hedonic treadmill'. Being promoted makes you happy (and being fired makes you sad); however, in less than three months, major events such as these lose their impact on happiness. The second myth is that wealth makes you happy. In very poor countries, being rich does predict greater wellbeing; however, in wealthier countries – except for the very poor, who are lower in happiness – once a person is comfortable, increases in wealth make little difference. The third myth is that good-looking people must be happier. Again, this is a myth: like wealth, attractiveness has little effect on happiness at all. Also, objective physical health is barely correlated with happiness; rather, it is our subjective view of how healthy we are that makes the difference.

A *World Happiness Report* has been published every year since 2012.[8] In the 2019 report, you can see the countries of the world listed on a scale of most to least happy over the period 2016–18. The top three on the list are:

---

[8] https://worldhappiness.report/ed/2019/changing-world-happiness.

1. Finland
2. Denmark
3. Norway.

The report uses several factors in its judgement of happiness, which can help us to consider how we operate organizations today. These factors and how they relate to businesses are shown in Table 7.2.

Table 7.2: Happiness factors and their relationship to business

Happiness report factors	Relationship to business
Positive affect: average frequency of happiness, laughter and enjoyment the previous day	Making sure you have a culture that acknowledges the importance of enjoyment at work, fun and laughter
Negative affect: average frequency of worry, sadness and anger the previous day	Being mindful of mental health issues at work, including stress and anxiety
Social support	Seeing the importance of social networks and workplace friendships
Freedom	Providing the right levels of autonomy in people's roles
Corruption	Running a business based on high levels of honesty, transparency and integrity

Generosity	Providing bonus and incentives schemes
Healthy life expectancy	Providing health and wellbeing programmes
GDP per capita	Providing the appropriate levels of salary across the organization

So what can we do to have happier lives and create happier organizations? Here's what research shows us:

1. *Make a habit of being kind to people.* Kindness exists in total engagement and in the loss of self-consciousness, and it gives you a longer-term feeling of happiness. The afterglow of pleasurable activities such as watching a movie, eating an ice cream or seeing friends is much shorter lived.

2. *Be optimistic.* This is sometimes easier said than done. The science shows you are either one or the other, but the key is that if you are a pessimist you can learn optimism and apply it. Scientists at the Mayo Clinic in Rochester, Minnesota selected 839 patients who came in for medical care. They all took a battery of tests, including one that looked at the trait of optimism. Of these patients, 200 had died by the year 2000. The optimists had 19% greater longevity. Optimists believe that setbacks are surmountable, whereas pessimists are up to eight times more likely to become depressed when bad events happen.

3. *Focus on building on your signature strengths* (those that come more naturally to you) and not on addressing your weaknesses.

4. *Find meaning in your life* (Dan Pink's purpose) that is attached to something larger than yourself; the larger the entity, the more meaning you will have in your life. The importance of creating and sharing the purpose of your business is therefore massively important.

5. *Aim to increase your own happiness.* Don't compete on happiness.

6. *Keep a gratitude journal.* Take five minutes a night before bed to write down what you are grateful for. Groups who have done this have found that their levels of joy, happiness and life satisfaction have shot up.

7. *Make life's pleasures habitual.* Find the optimal spacing in time for the pleasures you like in life (too often and they might well be an addiction).

8. *Savour life's pleasures.* Due to the speed of our lives, we so often rush through one thing to get onto the next. Fred B. Bryant and Joseph Veroff of Loyola University have studied the deliberate attention to the experience of pleasure (with echoes of Buddhism). This can be done in the moment as well as afterwards. Sharing a moment of pleasure from the past is the single strongest element of savouring – this can be relating an experience or sharing an image or a photo.

9. *Self-congratulation.* When others have said you are good at something or thanked you, then remind yourself about it. I keep the emails, letters and notes I've

received over the years that have thanked me for the support, coaching, mentoring and leadership insights I've given people. We need to remind ourselves that we really do make a difference to others in our own way.

10. *Sharpen perceptions and absorption.* Close your eyes when listening to music and let yourself be totally absorbed in the moment.

11. *Mindfulness.* With their origins in Buddhism, mindfulness and meditation are about slowing the mind down to be more attentive to the present.

In our businesses, money is losing its power and personal satisfaction is taking over. When I first went for a job at the age of 19, I was interested in a steady income and a job that wasn't too boring. How life has changed for me and for the world (thank goodness)! Job applicants want to know how satisfying the job will be for them, what the purpose, vision and values of the business are and what is said about the business on social media. People want more in life and we need to give it to them. This is not just about being great leaders; it is about having a social conscience and creating a better world. When we understand more about happiness, engagement and motivation, we become better people. Great leaders understand this and do it exceptionally well.

Engage the emotions

Questions for you and your leadership team

1. How well do you know what personally motivates your direct reports?
2. Do you create opportunities to encourage and praise your people daily (when appropriate)?
3. Do you give weekly feedback and monthly 121s with your direct reports?
4. Do you run staff surveys to understand how engaged and motivated your people are AND do you act on the results?
5. How much attention do you pay to creating a happy culture?

Chapter 8

Show grit

Passion and perseverance towards long-term goals.
– Dr Angela Duckworth

Introduction

Are you born with resilience or can you develop it on the journey through your life? The good news for all of us is that it is a bit of both. If our parents were extremely resilient, then there is a good chance that through our upbringing we have become resilient too, as they have been role models for us in that department. However, we can also develop resilience as we move through life; we can build it up over time.

'You are all stressed now!' That was the message from the keynote speaker I saw when I attended a Vistage Conference in London in 2018. Dr Tara Swart is one of the most prominent voices in neuroscience. Her point was that the world in which we now operate is so fast, so full of media messaging, apps, social media notifications and opportunities to compare ourselves (the way we look, the car we drive, the job we have) that our cortisol levels are running at an all-time high. As leaders, we must understand how to build up our own resilience or grit and that of our team. Becoming anxious and stressed is a sure path to illness, lack of productivity and days away from the office.

All over the world, mental health issues are on the rise. In a study conducted in the United States between 2006 and 2014, it was found that 8.3 million Americans (3.4% of the population) suffered from a serious mental health issue. At the same time, access to professional help is dwindling. In 2016 in the United Kingdom, over half a million employees reported experiencing stress, depression or anxiety, either caused or made worse by their job. That year, 12.5 million days were lost to organizations as a result. In the younger population (our next generation of workers), one in eight people reported mental health problems in 2014.[1]

In all the years I've been working with chief executives and leaders in both large corporations and the SME community, I've been able to see at first hand the stresses and strains that these business leaders and entrepreneurs are under. So what's the answer? People know that if they want to lose weight, get fitter and eat better, there are lots of available gyms, groups and self-help books. We feel less able to talk about our *mental* wellbeing: it is harder to know what to do and how to find what you need. Thank goodness mental health discussions are becoming more commonplace now and we seem to be turning a corner. However, there is still relatively little talked about in the general media about what we can do to help ourselves and at the same time there is a rise in prescriptions for antidepressant medications.

---

[1] NHS Digital: Mental Health of Children and Young People Survey, 2014.

This chapter looks at what we can do to help ourselves to become more resilient, to face the challenging world that presents itself to us every day and, with a growth mindset, face our world with more grit, moving from just surviving to thriving.

Understanding grit

Dr Angela Duckworth stood on the TED stage in April 2013 and delivered a six-minute talk entitled 'Grit: The Power of Passion and Perseverance',[2] which as of July 2020 had been seen by almost 22 million people. Her talk tackles this fascinating subject of grit and mental resilience. After some time as a McKinsey's consultant and a teacher, Duckworth trained to become a psychologist. What she found was that those with the most obvious talent (IQ) were not those who necessarily did the best in life, passed the most exams and succeeded. She worked at West Point Military Academy with cadets, trying to figure out who would stay and who would drop out; she studied children at the National Spelling Bee to see who would advance the most; and she looked inside businesses to see which salespeople would earn the most money and keep their jobs the longest. For those who were the most successful, one characteristic emerged: grit. Duckworth's definition of grit is 'passion and perseverance towards long-term goals'. It's about sticking with your future. Duckworth concluded that success has little to do with talent because grit

---

[2] See www.ted.com/talks/angela_lee_duckworth_grit_the_power_of_passion_and_perseverance?language=en.

matters more than talent. While we can always find exceptions, that's just what they are – exceptions. When we peel the layers of those we see as incredibly talented, we often find that they have put in the 10,000 hours of preparation. The idea of the 10,000 hours was originally written about in a 1993 paper written by Anders Ericsson, a Professor at the University of Colorado, called 'The Role of Deliberate Practice in the Acquisition of Expert Performance' and later brought to the masses in Malcolm Gladwell's book *Outliers*.[3]

It is often thought that people who achieve extraordinary things in their lives are born to the right parents or had a huge amount of luck. For a few that might be the case, but for the vast majority it's about hard work. Jim Collins said that we all get roughly the same amount of luck over our lifetimes and it is what we do with it that counts – he refers to this as a 'return on luck'. Grit is part genetics and part upbringing.

Let's take the example of Steve Jobs. Born in 1955 and adopted, he was brought up by a loving lower middle-class family. He found school boring, but his parents wanted to save and send him to college so he went. He then dropped out of Reed College in 1972. Meeting up with Steve Wozniak, he started Apple in his father's garage in 1976 and through long hours, determination and skill had made his first million dollars two years later at the age of 23. That same year, 1978, he split with his long-time girlfriend, Chrisann Brennan, and had his first computer flop in the Apple Lisa (named after his daughter). In 1984 he launched the Macintosh computer,

---

[3] Malcolm Gladwell, *Outliers: The Story of Success*, 2008.

which was a huge success, but later that year he was forced out of Apple by John Scully, the CEO he had brought in.

That first period in Apple saw an arrogant, opinionated and forceful Jobs, who was probably a hard person to be around. After he was forced out of Apple, he founded Next computers in 1985. Next produced high-end sophisticated computers that were extremely expensive and as a result he sold relatively few. With Next running out of money, he found Ross Perot, a billionaire investor, who injected the necessary funds. In 1986, Jobs then turned his creativity elsewhere and invested $10 million dollars in a failing Pixar, throwing all his creativity, marketing and sales skills at turning it around. His computer company, Next, moved out of its failing hardware and moved to software only, creating the basis for a stunning operating system, which Apple then bought to turn into iOS. Pixar would go on to make *Toy Story* and many more blockbusters, giving Jobs a huge return on his investment.

Jobs was, of course, asked back into Apple and the 'Jobs 2.0' version was created. When he returned to Apple, we saw a more rounded individual, battle scarred from the knocks he had taken and smarter with the learning and growth that had taken place. Jobs refocused Apple on a limited number of core products and, with his amazing partnership (and friendship) with Apple's chief designer Jony Ive, went on to bring to market the iMac, the iPod, iTunes, the iPhone and the iPad. Oh, and Pixar was sold to Disney in 2006 for $7.46 billion. All this from a kid who had started a business out of his dad's garage. When Jobs died of pancreatic cancer in 2011, aged 56, he was worth an estimated $10 billion. Jobs famously said that he was convinced that half of what separates successful

entrepreneurs from the non-successful ones is pure perseverance. He had grit in spades, but how did he cope with stress?
Did he move out of stretch and into stress? Did it cause his
cancer? We will never know, but we can look at techniques
to help ourselves deal with the stress we will face in our lives
today.

If grit is about passion and perseverance towards long
term goals (as Duckworth says), then we need to be pretty
sure what we are doing is significant enough that we really
want to do it. There are times we might start something
because it seems like a good idea, but we shouldn't be afraid to
stop it if it doesn't work for us. Just because we have invested
time and effort so far doesn't mean we have to continue if
we have figured out we just don't have the passion for it, or it
just doesn't help us move in the direction we want to. I took
up the clarinet about 25 years ago. I learnt how to play a few
tunes and to read music, but then I realized I didn't have the
passion to continue. I found out I didn't want to take it any
further, and had no ambition to be in a band or orchestra, so
I left it there. Was it a good idea to do it? Sure it was. I learnt
something and now know it's not for me. As Mark Twain
said, 'Twenty years from now you will be more disappointed
by the things you didn't do than by the ones you did.' At least
I had a go.

Becoming grittier

So what are the pieces that make up the grit puzzle and
what can we do to adopt some of these practices to help us
all become grittier? Grit is primarily about resilience, so let's

start there. What can we do to build resilience in ourselves and our teams? Here are 10 practical areas on which we can all focus to become grittier.

1. Find your purpose

As the quote by Nietzsche at the beginning of Chapter 1 says, 'He who has a why to live for can bear almost any how.'[4] As human beings, we are hard-wired to look for meaning in our lives. Some of us, from an early age, decide we want to become doctors or nurses, paramedics, join the fire or police service or do voluntary work. But the rest of us must search for meaning. If you look back at Chapter 1, you can see how models such as the Japanese *Ikigai* can help us. We know we have found our purpose when what we are doing is bigger than we are, when we don't see it as a job anymore, when there is no issue about working longer hours because we love what we do. Our life then becomes one life. I can't stand the term 'work–life balance' because it infers that work is somehow different from life! When you love your work (and that must be our aim), it becomes a case of balancing our 'work' with other things in life that are equally important to us, such as family life, health and wellbeing. I have only really felt totally fulfilled since starting my own business in 2006. Before that, I did a lot of things that I loved and some things that I really didn't, for some people I respected and some I didn't. I can now feel confident that while I will continue to learn, grow

---

[4] Friedrich Nietzsche (1844–1900), German philosopher, essayist and cultural critic.

and develop, every day I am also developing and inspiring leadership in others. I gain deep satisfaction when someone in one of my leadership workshops or keynotes gives me feedback that I have changed something for the better in their lives or when someone I have coached goes on to find their purpose too.

2. Create a personal vision

A vision or set of goals that you really want to achieve drives you on and will drive your team on if they have all bought in. It's all about motivation or passion, as Angela Duckworth says. When I ran a trail marathon, it was not at all pleasant past the 20-mile point. Every part of my body hurt and was telling me to stop, but my goal was not just to do my best, but to complete it. All that training I had done would be for nothing if I did not cross the line. I had also told many people and had raised sponsorship for a great charity – I could not let the charity down or have my friends see me as someone who couldn't go the distance. The goal was compelling, and the motivation was strong. I had the resilience to push through and succeed.

3. The power visualization

Athletes are brilliant at this, and so are actors. It is now becoming much more mainstream for people to adopt this approach in their everyday lives. Athletes will visualize the perfect golf swing, how the ball flies through the air landing perfectly on the green. The English women's hockey team penalty taker visualizes the perfect shot into the top corner and Sam Warburton, the captain of Wales and the Lions RFU team would visualize the hits he would make on the opposition, how he would push them back and how that would lift his team. Understanding the mental advantage in competition has enabled us to look into visualization and other techniques in a new way. Great golfers must positively visualize the perfect shot landing on the green and not the negative thought of making sure it doesn't land in the lake. Once the negative thought of 'avoid the lake, avoid the lake' gets into your head, all you can think about is the lake!

The same principles apply in the business world. When you are about to run a meeting or present to an audience, you need to visualize the meeting going extraordinarily well and at the end of the presentation you can 'see' the audience clapping and applauding you. This mental discipline will give you the maximum chance of showing up at your best and will over time become a habit. Of course, the precursor to delivering an amazing presentation is a lot of preparation, knowledge of the subject and developing ever better skills over time.

In 1995, Pascual-Leone carried out some experiments with a group of volunteers at Harvard Medical School. The first group practised a basic five-finger piano exercise for two hours a day over a five-day period. After the exercises, the volunteers were wired up to a transcranial magnetic stimulation (TMS). The researchers noticed that the brain was laying down new neural pathways. This was nothing new, as it was thought that by practising something new neural pathways would be created and then they would be there the next time (in our memory). The most amazing thing happened with the second group. They were asked to do the same thing, but with one major difference – they had no piano! They just had to visualize playing the five-finger routine. The TMS scans were then repeated and researchers found that exactly the same neural pathways had been created in the brain. This shows that we can improve what we do and develop a behaviour just through the power of visualization!

4. Develop a great support and challenge network

American author, entrepreneur and motivational speaker Jim Rohn famously said that we become the average of the six people we hang out with the most – so who are you hanging out with? We look at children when they are growing up and we are quite rightly concerned about who they are hanging out with in the playground or after school, because we don't want them to get into the 'wrong crowd', as we know it will influence them in the wrong way. When we grow up, the same applies. The people with whom we spend most of our time have an influence on us. Are we stretched and challenged by the conversations we have with our peers at work and our friends outside work, or are we left unstimulated and slightly bored by them? Does our support network reach out to help and support us when we need them, and do they help us get through challenging times, or do they tell us we are pushing ourselves too far for our own good and should embark on something simpler and less taxing?

A great support network can have an amazing influence on our lives allowing us to reach out when we have a challenge or opportunity about which we are unsure. Business coaches and mentors, our peers, an amazing boss and our friends should help us to build our confidence, validate our thinking, challenge us to go further and help us to build our resilience.

5. Be an optimistic realist

When you are faced with a challenge, what's your natural reaction? Is it, 'Yes I'm sure I can make a go of that'? Or is it, 'That looks really hard, I'm more than likely to screw it up, so I'll leave it this time'? As the saying goes, 'If you think you can, or you think you can't, then you are probably right!' Optimistic people believe they can achieve more than pessimistic people, which means that the incidences of them achieving more are going to be higher.

In Chapter 1, I mentioned *The Blue Zones*,[5] a book written by Dan Buettner and *National Geographic* about the people who live the longest in the world. The book identifies five regions that have the most centenarians on earth. Each Blue Zone has nine things in common and in addition to purpose (mentioned in Chapter 1), and the most obvious such as a mainly vegetarian-based diet and consistent levels of exercise, the people who they studied also believed they would live to a ripe old age – and they did!

At times, though, it can be argued that realism will see you through difficult times, more than just pure optimism. In his book *Good to Great*, Jim Collins explains the Stockdale

---

[5] Dan Buettner, *The Blue Zones: 9 Lessons for Living Longer from the People Who Live the Longest*, 2009.

paradox.[6] Admiral Jim Stockdale was the highest-ranking American prisoner during the Vietnam War, held in what was known as the 'Hanoi Hilton'. He was regularly tortured during his eight years of captivity (1965–73). He did everything to try to keep up the spirits of his fellow inmates. When Collins met Stockdale, he asked him how he dealt with the misery and not knowing what would happen to him. Stockdale said he never doubted that he would get out and turn the experience into the defining event of his life. When Collins asked him who didn't get out, he said, 'That was easy – it was the optimists. They always thought they would be out by Christmas. When Christmas came and went and they weren't out, their hopes were shattered and they died of a broken heart.' Stockdale went on to say that we should never confuse faith that you will prevail with the discipline to confront the brutal facts.

These two approaches can seem contradictory, but I don't see them that way. To be resilient, you must accept the situation you are in and you must believe you can and will get through (that's the positivity and optimism), and you shouldn't believe that it's going to be quick or easy. The toughest challenges in our lives won't be either of those things.

6. Embrace change

This is probably the most obvious and most written about way to build resilience in yourself. When we stay inside our

---

[6] Jim Collins, *Good to Great*, 2001.

comfort zone, we avoid challenge, discomfort and potential failure and as a result miss the opportunity to learn, grow and stretch ourselves. Challenging ourselves to step outside our comfort zone shows us that we can do it and we can then push ourselves even further. Change then becomes a habit, a virtuous circle. We start to look for more challenges in our life that will stretch and grow us, and move us along the path towards our vision, while realizing our purpose. The more we challenge ourselves, the easier and more of a habit it becomes. We know when we face a challenge that it might not go perfectly, but we win some and we lose some, and our resilience grows.

7. Lose more often

It might sound odd, but winners are actually losers! What I mean by this is that to win and to keep winning and be the best, you must keep stretching and pushing yourself with the inevitable outcome that you will lose along the way. The most famous and successful basketball player of all time, Michael Jordon, said:

> I've missed more than 9000 shots in my career, I've lost almost 300 games. 26 times I've been trusted to take the game winning shot and missed. I've failed over and over again in my life. *And that is why I succeed.*
>
> – Michael Jordon

When you lose, you build up your mental fortitude. As one of my clients said to me, you build up 'personal proof points'. In other words, if I can do that, or cope with that, or recover from that, then I can certainly do this thing! One of the problems that we have created in many cultures and societies in recent decades is in our schooling system, where it has become the norm to give our children praise simply for taking part – the 'we are all winners' approach. The facts of life are that failure is a part of it and our kids need to learn this lesson from an early age. What we need to learn is that it is okay to fail and that's the source of much of our learning and life skill development. Great sports teams come off the pitch, even when they've won, and analyse what they didn't do well, as well as what they did well. In business, we want our people to take risks – that's how we progress and that's how they grow. With risks come rewards and failures, as Michael Jordan so eloquently put it. Life is so much easier when we realize that it's just a normal part of our journey.

8. Choose your response

A friend of mine once said to me, 'Respond, don't react'. For extroverts, this is a bigger challenge than it is for introverts. Extroverts think and speak at the same time (as opposed to an introvert like me who thinks it through first before saying what they think), and therefore it is harder for a natural extrovert to pause and not react straight away to what happens to them. But we all know that is not always the best way to deal with a situation. When someone criticizes you for something you've done, the danger is that your 'inner chimp' takes over and your ego steps in. The chimp model is described in Professor Steve Peters' book, *The Chimp Para-*

dox.[7] He describes our inner chimp as the emotional team within our brain that thinks and acts for us without our permission. What happens is that our blood pressure rises, and we start to defend our position and even attack the other person's position. It becomes a win–lose battle! The response, rather than the reaction, says we take control of the situation and our emotions. We put in a two- to three-second pause and we say, 'I never thought of it that way. Tell me more about your thinking.' This then becomes a more reasoned response. It allows us to learn new things, explore what we have in common, discuss our differences and agree on a way forward. This more reasoned response keeps our blood pressure down. As Dr Stephen R. Covey said, 'Most people do not listen with the intent to understand; they listen with the intent to reply.'[8]

9. Focus on what you can control

Too often, you hear people getting very anxious about things over which they simply have no control. If you focus on what you can control and influence, then you can act. However, if you focus on what you can't control and influence, you are literally powerless, which can lead to anxiety, frustration and stress. For example, we can't control how the economy of our country is doing if there has been a global pandemic.

---

[7] Steve Peters, *The Chimp Paradox: The Mind Management Programme for Confidence, Happiness and Success*, 2012.
[8] Stephen R. Covey, *The Seven Habits of Highly Effective People*, 1989.

We can't control who the head of a political party is or (apart from our vote) who gets elected to be prime minister or president. We can't control how our football team performs at the weekend or whether our idol at the decathlon performs well at the Olympics. We can influence several things, but not control them – for example, the relationships we have with our friends and loved ones and our team at work, what we eat and the effect it has on our health, and even our pets (to some extent!). What we can control is how much effort we put into our job, how and when we practise for something we love to do, our response to someone who says something with which we disagree and the effort we put into anything we do. Figure 8.1 shows this with examples.

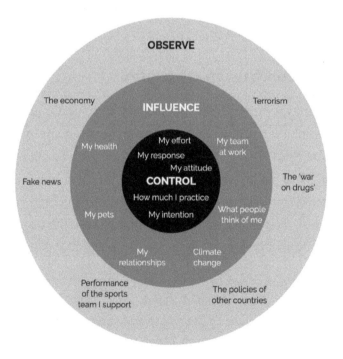

Figure 8.1: Control, influence and observe model

Focus on what you can control and take action to control it. Be honest about the influence you have on things you don't control and, if they don't work, don't worry too much if you've done your best, and don't stress about things you can only observe.

10. Be disciplined and build routines

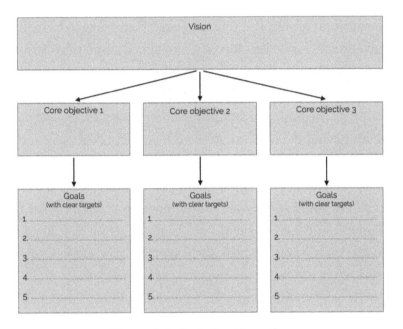

Figure 8.2: 1–3–5 action plan

Whether it is writing a book, going to the gym or brushing our teeth, we need routines and discipline to keep them going. I use various techniques to build my routines and stick to them. First, I need to make sense of them in the bigger picture of where I'm heading (my personal vision). Then I need to set myself goals and targets. Third, I need to tell people what they are (make them public) and fourth, I need to make it as easy for myself as I can to ensure they happen. For the first of these three techniques, I use a great framework called a 1–3–5 action plan (Figure 8.2), shared with me by Pete Wilkinson, founder and CEO of Reclaro.[9] It is explained in his very practical book, *Unstoppable*.[10] I have now used this framework for three years.

By using this framework and sharing it with my wife and the business groups I run, I know what I am going to be held accountable for. It also forces me to spend some time 'strategically' planning what I am going to achieve in the next 12 months, seeing how I will be stretched and what I will need to learn. The fourth technique, making it easy for myself, is about having the tools to do the job (which takes away any excuses you might want to use), building everything into my diary (including writing, bike riding and working out, as well as all my business activities) and preparing ahead for what I want to do. For example, if I am going to get up at 6.30 am and go on my exercise bike, I will set my alarm and have my kit ready in the bathroom to put on as soon as I rise.

To achieve things in your life, you will need resilience; some will be built-in to your circuitry and hard-wired from your DNA, and some you can make the choice to build in yourself. It is so important to be able to withstand the inevitable knocks you will take in your life on the journey you

---

[9] See www.reclaro.com.

[10] Pete Wilkinson, *Unstoppable: Using the Power of Focus to Take Action and Achieve Your Goals*, 2014.

have set out, so take these on board and bring these techniques into your work teams and your personal life too.

Show grit

Questions for you and your leadership team

1. How resilient are you and how resilient is your leadership team?
2. How focused are you on pursuing the long game when short-term challenges arise?
3. Do you look for grit in the people you hire?
4. Do you help your people to become grittier?
5. How closely do you monitor and support the mental health of your people?

Summary of Part 2

We have now covered the first two parts of *The Leadership Map*. In Part 1, we laid the foundations for any business: the decision filters of purpose, vision (unreasonable dream), values and strategy. In Part 2, we discovered how to work with your people and teams: challenging the status quo, building dream teams, engaging and motivating them and finally building grit and resilience. In Part 3, we will address the fundamentals of executing your strategy: embedding the optimal structure, developing your strategic priorities, measuring success and finally running great meetings.

PART 3
Strategy execution

Chapter 9

Create the optimal structure

Structure supports the execution of your strategy.

Introduction

The structure of your organization needs to support not only your strategy (competitive advantage) but also your culture. It is not just a practical way of organizing the workplace; it is a way of enabling great communications and teamwork and distributing power through the organization to make the most of every person. The wrong structure will mean the development of silos (business divisions that operate independently and avoid sharing information); communication then breaks down and the egos of the powerful are enhanced, while the confidence of the powerless diminishes. Power doesn't need to be a zero-sum game. At the heart of most successful organizations is the ability of people to make the right decisions at the right time. The right structure for your business, coupled with great leadership and culture, will enable this to happen.

Workplaces are changing, and workplace design is changing too, with companies such as London-based Peldon

Rose[1] leading the way in design-led environments that fit the culture and strategy of their clients. Our employees want to work in different ways than in the past. Gallup's *State of the American Manager* 2018 showed us just how much these things are changing:

- *When you work.* More flexible work time – 52% of employees say they have some choice over when they work.
- *How you work.* Technology is the #1 enabler of smart and mobile working in and out of the office.
- *Where you work.* More remote working – 43% of employees work away from their team at least some of the time; flexible spaces that rethink the way we live and work.
- *De-stressing work.* Increased emphasis on wellbeing and biophilic design (green space and nature impact mental health positively).

The global Coronavirus pandemic of 2020 accelerated these trends and forced leaders to look at their workspaces, their organizational structures and their culture to ask themselves some questions: What is the purpose of having office space? What should our office design be? What's the right balance between home working and office working? What's the opportunity now with video conferencing (now that we've made it work)? The purpose of office space, as defined by Jitesh Patel (JP) CEO of Peldon Rose, is threefold:

---

[1] Peldon Rose Office Design, www.peldonrose.com.

1. It's the heart of collaboration.
2. It's a learning institution (including coaching and mentoring).
3. It's a social interface.

Workplace environments are changing to match more of the way we might live at home. Entrance areas are becoming coffee shops, lounge areas and communal lunch areas with large tables designed to throw people together to talk. Small private rooms are being built as well as larger team working rooms to allow for introverts to find private places to work and think away from louder, more direct extroverts. Spaces for bikes are provided as a matter of course. Healthier food and drinks are being provided to entice people into the communal canteens. Cross-functional 'lunch and learns' and internal academies are springing up to bring people together out of their functional teams. More leaders are having their lunch at the communal tables to talk and listen to their employees. There is no doubt that we need to understand and implement the latest thinking on how we physically design our offices as well as consider how we design organizational structures that enable the delivery of our strategy and create amazing cultures that we want to be a part of and that people want to join.

Finding the right structure

The structure of your organization has probably not been something you have thought about a lot, but there is not much written about it and only limited understanding of what the options and opportunities are. If you use Microsoft PowerPoint and you want an icon for structure it will only give you a hierarchical structure, which starts with the leader at the top, followed by a top team in the layer below who manage different departments. Familiar? This may be the perfect and most optimal structure for your business, but equally it may not.

The right structure for your business will:

- allow your people to play to all their strengths
- allow people – especially managers – to be held accountable for their actions and results as well as for their teams
- enable organizations to communicate well across, within and between departments, divisions and regions
- enable optimal decision-making in the right places at the right time
- support a culture of cooperation and teamwork
- support the execution of your strategy
- enable people to be stretched and challenged, and to grow.

If your organizational culture does not score well on these criteria, then you probably don't have the optimal structure in your business today.

The problem when you get the structure wrong is that people go into silos, accountability gets diluted or lost, communication breaks down or is non-existent and people develop only in narrow areas of expertise and then defend their area. The culture of the business suffers, teamwork is lost and people fight from their corner rather than live their purpose. Ultimately, the structure fights against the execution of the strategy.

This chapter will look at several organizational structures, some of which you will be familiar with and may have worked in, others probably less so. You need to figure out what will suit your business best. It may be one or other of the main ones I describe, or it may be a hybrid of two or more. I want you to think about it and make a conscious decision about the structure you adopt and how well it works for you. As well as organization structure, I will also look at how you structure your own job, within an organization – for example, how you spend your time. I will also give you a number of tools to help you look at how you do this now and what to think about for the future. You see, we must design organizations and the jobs within them for the future, not just the present.

The hierarchy

The first and most common organizational structure is the hierarchy (Figure 9.1). As I've said above, in PowerPoint you can find a hierarchy to insert into a presentation, making it easy to insert names, functions and job roles. It's our default and has been around forever. What it shows is one person or team reporting upwards to another. It states clearly who manages and reports to whom and exactly what everyone does. It allows for very clear reporting lines and a real focus in people's jobs. If I am in the marketing function, I can be really focused on marketing and I can look to progress further up the ladder with promotions. There will be very clear measures and targets for each department and job role.

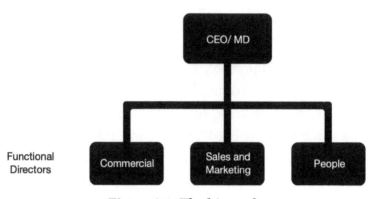

Figure 9.1: The hierarchy

It does have some drawbacks, of course – as do all organizational structures. It can create silos between departments, and even competition, with one not knowing (or sometimes caring) what the other is doing. A hierarchy is, of course, a triangle, so the further up you go, the narrower it becomes. This means you are bound to lose good people along the way who you simply can't promote further up the ladder. With hierarchies, you need to create specialist jobs that will allow people to become experts in certain areas, so they can still be motivated to stay with you over time.

The matrix

Following on naturally from the hierarchy is the matrix structure (Figure 9.2), which takes all the pros and cons of the hierarchy and adds in further focus and some further complexity. The matrix is a natural progression for many companies when they expand into new geographies, create project groups or introduce product lines. They create shared support functions that offer their services to the different work groups or geographic regions, such as HR, IT and marketing.

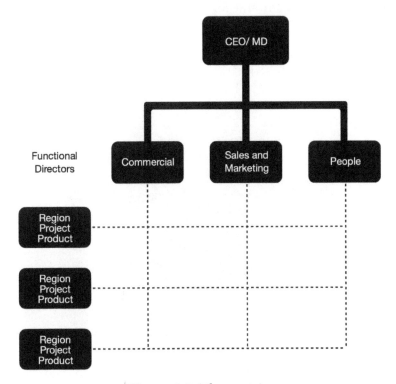

Figure 9.2: The matrix

This can indeed create a useful team focus for the dedicated project or product teams with the knowledge that they don't need their own HR or IT but still have support from those functions. However, as organizations get bigger – especially, in my experience, with geographic expansion – they can develop duplicate roles in a country as well as in the head office support functions. The other problem that matrix structures can throw up is dual reporting lines – people can get pulled in two directions. For example, I am a sales executive reporting to the head of sales and working within a product team, or I am an HR executive working for the head office support team and for the head of a geographic area such as Asia.

Core Plus

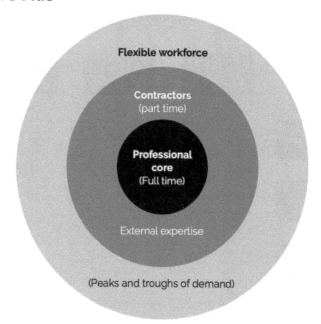

Figure 9.3: Core Plus

Core Plus (Figure 9.3) is where most start-up businesses begin and many, for obvious reasons, decide to continue with this very flexible structure.

Many professional services firms adopt this kind of structure, which allows them to employ specialist staff in key roles for projects. At the end of the project, the member of staff finishes their contract and either moves to another client or takes a break. The contractors will often command a premium day rate as they only earn when they work, but the plus is that they are 'sharpening their sword' constantly through experience on different projects with different clients. The best contractors are in high demand and clients are often looking to recruit them in-house. There is always a chance, therefore, that they are offered a job with a client and the next time you want them they may be off the market.

In addition to the contractors, some companies also have another circle of flexible workforce. While contractors are highly paid and may have long-term relationships with their clients over many years (on a part-time basis), the next circle, called the flexible workforce, may only be required during a busy period – for example, Christmas – to cope with demand. In an event management company, a flexible workforce may be required when the company is on site, producing and managing the event; for that limited time, a stage builder, lighting specialists, camera operators and so on will be required.

One of the drawbacks of this structure is that it can be difficult to develop an organizational culture with people constantly coming and going. It relies on a very strong core and ruthless selection of top experts in the contractor and flexible workforce circles.

Dynamic

Dynamic is the most modern of the structures and in many ways the most radical. Self-managed teams have, of course, been around for a long time in different guises; in Japan, they became quality circles and continuous improvement efforts, in the United States they were known as 'innovation task forces' and in Europe they were originally referred to as 'participation management'.

Patagonia is an example of what Frederic Laloux, in his book *Reinventing Organizations*,[2] calls a Teal organization. Teal is a successful American clothing company with an employee churn of only 4–4.5%, which is unheard of in the industry. A Teal organization is one that is a living organism or system that is 'purpose driven', and that has self-management and 'wholeness' – bringing your whole self to work. These foundations are difficult to argue with. Patagonia was founded in 1973 by Yvon Chouinard in California. An accomplished rock climber, Yvon wanted better equipment to fuel his passion and supply a growing demand. Patagonia is different, as its mission (or purpose) states: 'At Patagonia we appreciate that all life on earth is under threat of extinction. We aim to use the resources we have – our business, our investments, our voice and our imagination – to do something about it.'

Patagonia has a flat structure, describing it more like a network than a structure, with no reverence for traditional

[2] Frederic Laloux, *Reinventing Organizations: A Guide to Creating Organizations Inspired by the Next Stage of Human Consciousness*, 2014.

hierarchies. The company's philosophy is that the manager is more of a mentor and a resource, providing coaching and direction, assuring that the work is aligned to the highest business priorities. People then have full autonomy to get on and do the work. It is clear to see how structure and culture go hand in hand in Patagonia. The company hires independent people who set their own schedules with complete flexibility. There is no annual performance rating; Patagonia wants its managers to be coach rather than judge. No meetings are scheduled at lunch, as they value people's time to do yoga or running or whatever they need to do. They describe the biggest challenge as decision-making, which is obvious when it lies in a hierarchy, but less obvious in a network.

Decision-making was at the heart of Captain David Marquet's leadership philosophy, 'intent-based leadership', which he described in his book *Turn the Ship Around*.[3] Marquet graduated at the top of his class from the US Naval Academy and joined the submarine force. He was never entirely comfortable with the traditional leader-following model, where the goal of leader is to influence people to comply rather than think. Ultimately, he had the chance to put his intent-based leadership ideas into practice because he was forced to. He was unexpectedly diverted from becoming captain of the *USS Olympia* (a position for which he had spent 12 months preparing) to command the *USS Santa Fe* when its captain quit. The *Santa Fe* was the worst performing submarine in the US fleet, and Marquet had two weeks to

---

[3] David Marquet, *Turn the Ship Around: The True Story of Turning Followers into Leaders*, 2012.

prepare to take command, initially knowing little about the *Santa Fe* or its crew. When I met Marquet and heard him talk about his journey at a Vistage conference in London, it centred around an amusing and quite scary story.

Less than four weeks into his new job on the *Santa Fe*, Captain Marquet was running a drill to simulate a fault with the reactor. The drill is designed to challenge and stress the crew. The propulsion of the submarine is shifted from the main engines to a smaller electric propulsion motor and, as Marquet points out, has the same proportions as driving your car with your electric toothbrush! During the exercise, Marquet decided to speed up the electric motor, which would drain the battery quicker (putting more pressure on the crew to find the fault with the reactor and fix it quickly). He ordered 'Ahead two thirds', which was the order that was commonplace on the *USS Olympia*, on which he had been trained. Nothing happened. He asked the crew member operating the controls what had happened, and the crew member replied, 'Captain, on this submarine we only have one third on the electric motor.' This was the key moment for Marquet. He didn't know the ship like the men did, so it was literally unsafe for him to give the orders. They turned it around. His crew stopped bringing him problems without solutions and started with intentions. They would approach Marquet with the words 'I intend to'. This shifted the responsibility and ownership squarely onto his team. He would ask questions about the situation, to understand, then ultimately ask his team to carry on. Things started shifting, decisions started to be taken throughout the submarine where they needed to be taken, leadership changed from leader–follower to leader–leader. The *USS Santa Fe* went from being the worst performing submarine to the best performing submarine in the US Navy.

Holacracy

Let's now look at an organizational structure called holacracy, which has been developed and codified by Brian Robertson, the CEO of Holacracy.org. It is almost certainly the most complete system for a dynamic structure. Most famously, holacracy has been implemented by Zappos, the US online shoe and clothing retailer, based in Las Vegas, bought by Amazon for $1.2 billion in 2009. Holacracy is now practised by over 1000 companies around the world and has over 2500 practitioners who can help you to implement it! Zappos describes it as a pre-built, 'out of the box' solution that it could implement, without having to make something up that would fit. Zappos' reason for changing was the same one that most organizations might use – a frustration that as you grow, more layers are introduced and decision-making slows down or grinds to a halt.

A holacratic structure (Figure 9.4) is based around the principle of getting the most out of your people, providing self-management with several roles per person and broad scopes of authority. Any semblance of command and control, or even management, is lost. When Zappos implemented it in 2014, it actually lost 18% of its workforce, who didn't like the idea. Jordan Sams, a team leader with Zappos during the transition, was nervous when it was announced, but as it was implemented he discovered, 'We had to become faster and more frequently innovative than we'd been in the prior few years and holacracy was seen as a route towards us being able to do so.' Full-blown holacracy may not be for everyone, but the core concepts are difficult to argue with.

> *We had to become faster and more frequently innovative than we'd been in the prior few years and holacracy was seen as a route towards us being able to do so.*
> — *Jordan Sams, team leader with Zappos*

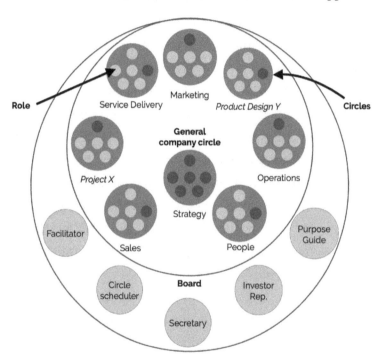

Figure 9.4: A holacratic structure

Between 1996 and 2006, I ran the UK offices of Celemi, a Swedish-based global learning and change business with a philosophy based on pedagogy (the science of learning). I remember speaking with Klas Mellander, the founder and author of *The Power of Learning*,[4] which sits at the heart of the Celemi model – we were talking about organizational structure and associated culture. We concluded that there is a spectrum of cultures and associated structures; at one end are rules-based cultures that are very structured with clear rules established for everything the company does. You must know the rules and follow the rules – there is little room for creativity and new ideas. In this type of culture and structure, people look for the rules in order to know what they can and can't do. At the other end of the spectrum are values-based cultures, where the purpose or mission of the company along with the values provide the basis of all decision-making. Too far down one end of the spectrum and you can have chaos and too far down the other you can end up with robots! Holacracy is trying to do a bit of both; it is very purpose driven and is combined with a constitution and governance that provide the structure within which to operate.

Let me now explain holacracy in a bit more detail. In holacracy, everyone has a number of roles (not a job description), depending on the skills and experience they have, and these roles are transparent for anyone to see. If you want to know who is responsible for anything in the organization, you can simply look it up on the software platform they recommend. Roles are dynamic and will change as the organization changes. Decisions are taken locally and not passed up the chain for management to take – it's quicker and more agile. Only the people required to make a decision are involved.

---

[4] Klas Mellander, *The Power of Learning: Fostering Employee Growth*, 1993.

Our research and experience tell us that elements of self-organization will become valuable tools for companies of all kinds, yet we see real challenges in embracing the approach wholesale.

– Harvard Business Review, *July–August 2016*

Every role fits into a team, called a circle, and circles have their own purpose within the overall organizational purpose. Circles make decisions not only about what they do, but also about how they do it, so that they can improve the processes as they go along. Everyone has the responsibility to identify 'tensions'; these are challenges and opportunities for things to improve. These are brought to a governance meeting in the circle and proposals are made, then new ways trialled and, if successful, implemented. In holacracy, there are very clear rules and governance that support decision-making, but that is ultimately pushed down to the individual level within a circle and let's not forget that individuals can play multiple roles in the company, which can allow them greater personal growth potential.

In summary, there is no perfect structure; rather, there are pros and cons for all of them. As the above quote from the *Harvard Business Review* shows, holacracy isn't perfect either. What you must do is look for ideas from all these structures. Don't feel you have to be wedded to just one. Most organizations in which I have worked have created hybrid models, adopting the bits that best fit their purposes.

Most organizations and leaders pay little attention to structure. It's what they inherited, and they are not aware of the numerous options out there. Consider what kind of organization you need to be and find a structure that really supports your strategy. Perhaps you will take some elements of holacracy and combine them with a hierarchy creating a hybrid model. Find a structure that fits your culture, develops and grows your people and allows you to pivot quickly in a world that won't tolerate slow movers.

Role structure

There is one final area to cover in this chapter, which is role structure. All too often I have seen organizations grow and then plateau, partly due to the leader and the leadership team doing the same thing that they were doing when they were running a smaller business. The logic is that if the business is growing and changing, then your job role needs to adapt and change too. This also throws up the learning and growth in which all leaders must constantly be engaged so that they can perform at a different, higher level. It is a myth that leaders who start businesses can't grow them into large and even giant businesses – there are so many examples where this has happened: Branson (Virgin), Jobs (Apple) and Gates (Microsoft) are three with huge legacies and more recently Katrina Lake of Stitch Fix, Stefania Mallett of ezCator and Pat McGrath of Pat McGrath Labs have shown us how it can be done.

Figure 9.5 shows what happens over time as a business grows. Certain peaks are hit. Some leaders grow with the business while some fall behind, defaulting to the previous management positions or taking on more specialist functions. Bridging this gap requires an awareness of where you are, followed by motivation, belief and commitment to learning and growth. The journey to leadership is not for everybody – and nor should it be.

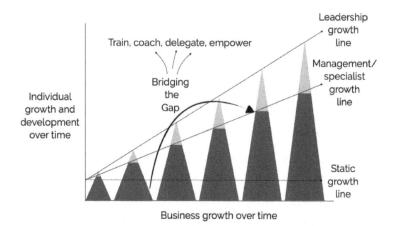

Figure 9.5: Bridging the leadership gap

Once you've realized that you need to grow, the challenge is to figure out what you need. That comes down to the demands of the business, your capability and confidence and where your passion lies. A simple model I use with leaders is to have them draw a circle, which represents 100% of how they spend their time. Now they must fill it in and share with me what that looks like. We then have a long conversation about whether that looks about right for their job role and what the company or department needs right now. More often than not, they find that their job needs to change. An example of how a leader typically might spend their time is shown in Figure 9.6.

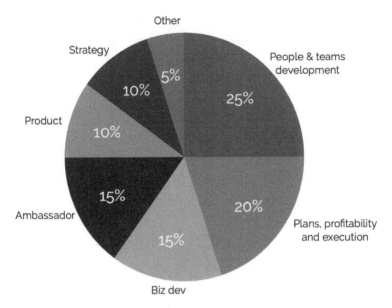

Figure 9.6: How leaders spend their time

So they draw a new circle with the new role that they need to occupy and the rough percentages of time they should spend on each of the constituent parts. Now the action to be taken is to decide what to do to move from the current circle or role to the new one. This will require an action planning process that involves learning new skills, delegating work to others and stopping some work that you just enjoy doing because it is in your comfort zone. Once you have created this new role for yourself, run this exercise across your whole team, so everyone knows what everyone else is doing with their time. Isn't that a great way to run a team?

The second way to use this model is as a planning tool for the future. If your business is growing at 10% a year and you are recruiting constantly, then the business is going to be a different shape in the coming years. Pick a year ahead, then two, then three. What will your role require then? It is too late to change the role when you get there, you need to start the process now so you are ahead of the curve and will not be left behind. I have run this process with two far-sighted and courageous owners/CEOs who decided they were simply not the right people to run their businesses in the future. They both found someone better in that role, and they took on a role that they wanted, that used their skills and experience to the maximum. Never confuse ownership of a business with being the CEO or MD.

As I said at the start of this chapter, structure is not something we discuss much in our businesses, yet it can make the difference between great communication and the development of organizational silos, accountability versus cop out, personal development and growth versus being stuck in a rut and ultimately a business failing to make the most of its people to deliver on its strategy.

Create the optimal structure

Questions for you and your leadership team

1. Does your senior leadership team understand the different organizational structures that are possible?
2. How well does your structure support your strategy?
3. How far through the business is personal accountability held?

4. How well does your structure enable your people to play to all their strengths?

5. How well does your structure enable great communication across all parts of your business?

Chapter 10

Plan your strategic priorities

Plan slowly and carefully and then be confident and swift in execution.

Introduction

Strategic priorities are the big goal that you want to achieve over a certain timescale, usually a year split over four quarters. As they are strategic, there should not be too many of them. Most great organizations with which I work have between six and eight, but no more, or they would just not be strategic.

I am often asked to run senior management team off-site workshops to help them put together their strategic priorities for the next year. When this is a new client, I ask them for four things, which are their 'decision filters' (Part 1 of this book) for all strategic decisions in their business:

1. your purpose – why is your business here? (see Chapter 1)
2. your vision – what is your 'unreasonable dream'? (see Chapter 2)
3. your core values (see Chapter 3)

4. your strategy (see Chapter 4).

The big 'aha' moment here for many leaders is how on earth they will be able to determine what their strategic priorities are for the following year unless they are able to hold them against the following questions:

1. Why is your business here?
2. Where do you want to be in the future?
3. How do you behave?
4. What makes you different?

✳ ✳ ✳

These four critical decision filters for your business, and particularly for your SLT, must be kept constantly at front of mind as you create your strategic priorities and then go on to execute them.

What's in a strategic priority?

A strategic priority is something that is critical to your business. It is strategic (not tactical); it has a fully developed plan; it involves key people in your business; it has a budget assigned to it; and someone at a senior level will be held accountable for its delivery.

Every strategic priority that is created in your business should follow the same format, whether it be a PowerPoint or Keynote presentation or a Word or Pages document. There should be an agreed set of headings that define the content. See below for a list of the headings I have found most useful:

Strategic priorities template

1. *Accountable person.* One person must be accountable for each strategic priority. Many people are likely to be responsible for delivery of the plan, but only one person must be held accountable for its creation, its delivery and reporting progress to the SLT on at least a monthly basis. Their name must be put against the strategic priority.

2. *Current reality.* This is the context for your plan. What are the critical assumptions underpinning your plan? What's the business environment looking like? Is it challenging, growing, declining? How did you do last year? Include four to six metrics describing the previous year. What did you learn? What can you do better this year? A SWOT or other strategic analysis tool can be useful here. The SWOT (described more fully in Chapter 4) is a tool to be run with the whole team and identifies both the strengths and weaknesses of the business (internal) as well as the opportunities and threats to the organization (externally). In a fast-changing environment, it is often a good idea to run this analysis every six months with your team. The external analysis often requires further research by one or two of your team before their findings are brought to the meeting.

3. *Strategic objectives.* What are the objectives for the year? These are the main accomplishments you will make by year's end. Include the key trends driving change in the business environment to which the business and your department must respond.

4. *Activities/actions.* What are the activities/actions you will take this year to achieve your objectives? Who is responsible for each of the actions and what are the measure and target? See Chapter 11 for Key Performance Indicators that should be included here.

5. *Time plan with key milestones, measures and targets.* This is a time plan spread over the 12 months of the year. The time plan will show when the actions start, key milestones on the way and when the action should be completed. Your monthly management meetings will look closely at how they are tracking and adjust accordingly. Many organizations use RAG (red, amber, green), also known as a traffic light rating, so they can quickly see what's on and off track.

6. *Resource allocation.* What resources are you going to need to implement the plan: money (see the next point), time, people, specific skills, technology, other stakeholders, etc.? Where will they come from? Are there currently the capability and capacity within the business? What are the hiring requirements within the year and when will they need to start?

7. *Budget.* What is the overall budget required for this strategic priority and when (by month) will it be used over the course of the year? If you are generating income (e.g. sales), then how is this forecast over the year?

8. *Interdependencies between strategic priorities.* During the annual planning process, all the draft strategic priorities must be shared, challenged and ultimately supported by the leadership team. During this process, it will be important to cross-check each

strategic priority against every other one, to understand interdependencies and to align actions and timescales (e.g. one may need to finish before another can start).

9. *Anticipated challenges, risks and mitigation.* What are the challenges and risks of this strategic priority? What could go wrong in delivery? What happens if it can't be completed? How will you mitigate any possible challenges that might occur?

Figure 10.1 shows a one-page strategic plan. While it is only one page, you may need to use a piece of A3 to fit it all on. It includes all parts of the strategic plan, as well as bringing in the four decision filters (in Part 1) that must form the platform for the plan.

Creating strategic priorities

Every business needs an annual planning process, not only to create but also to execute your strategy. See Chapter 12 for details of what needs to happen at the monthly strategic meetings, when you review progress against your strategic priorities. The planning process is crucial and needs to be spread over several months. One of the most impressive companies in this regard is Toyota; its approach is to plan slowly and carefully, create buy-in and understanding across the business, challenge thinking and then, when the final plans are agreed, it can be confident and swift in execution. If the planning is not done carefully, then problems will arise in the execution through the year.

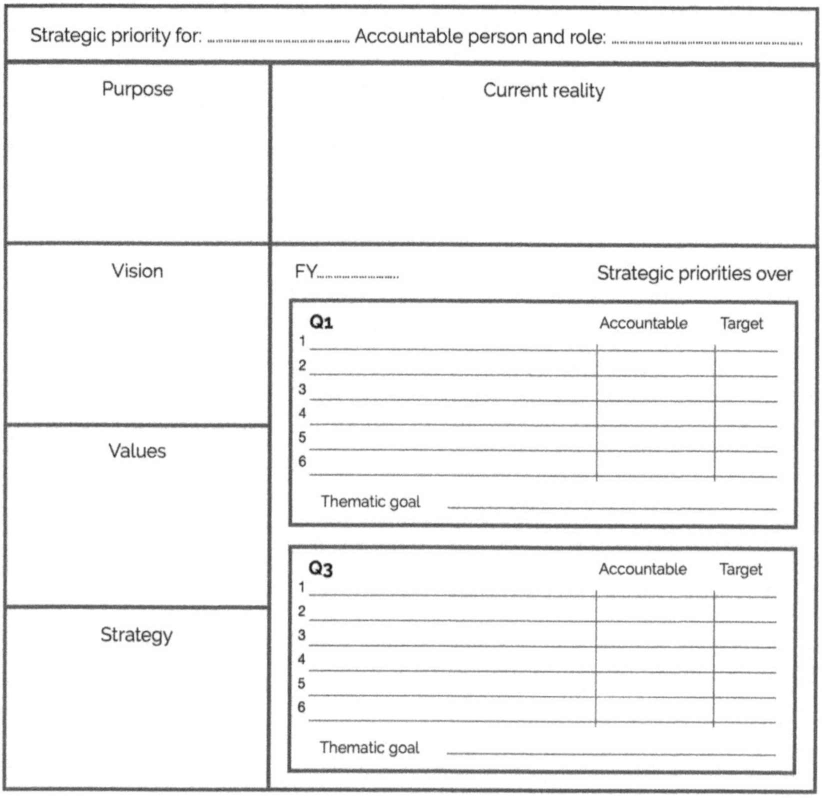

Strategic priority for: .... Accountable person and role: ....

Purpose	Current reality
Vision	FY............................ Strategic priorities over
	Q1 Accountable Target
	1
	2
	3
	4
Values	5
	6
	Thematic goal
	Q3 Accountable Target
	1
	2
Strategy	3
	4
	5
	6
	Thematic goal

Figure 10.1a: One-page strategic plan

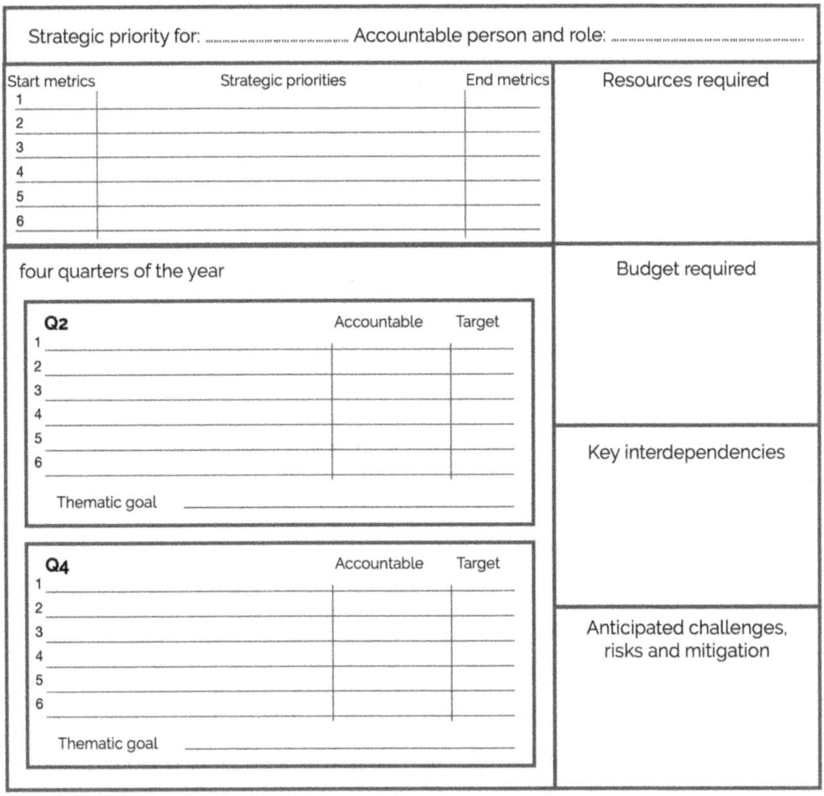

Strategic priority for: .... Accountable person and role:			
Start metrics	**Strategic priorities**	**End metrics**	**Resources required**
1			
2			
3			
4			
5			
6			

four quarters of the year

Q2   Accountable   Target
1
2
3
4
5
6

Thematic goal _____

Budget required

Key interdependencies

Q4   Accountable   Target
1
2
3
4
5
6

Thematic goal _____

Anticipated challenges, risks and mitigation

Figure 10.1b: One-page strategic plan

Your strategic priorities are set by the members of the senior leadership team. They should have received input from members of their teams to produce a first draft. It is essential that each member of the team hears and can critique every other plan. There are several reasons for this:

- It will make each plan stronger as it will mean they have been 'road tested' and challenged objectively.
- They are checked for alignment against the vision and overall KPIs of the business.
- Interdependencies are worked through between each strategic priority.
- Buy-in is created to other plans as well as your own (and incentive plans must support this).
- When presenting back progress at monthly strategic meetings, everyone knows where the other members of the senior leadership team should be, and can challenge and support them.

The senior leadership team is likely to have two or three iterations of its draft plans before agreeing and signing off the final set for communication to the business. They are created with one eye on your vision and strategy. If you have produced a three-year detailed vision, as laid out in Chapter 2 (this needs to be a rolling vision, updated annually), then the purpose of the strategic planning process is to produce a set of plans that will deliver on the first year of your vision, divided into four quarters and reported on monthly.

When presenting and creating your strategic priorities for the following year, you must be careful that you do not create too many. Be ambitious, but make sure that stretch is doable; otherwise you will just be disappointed. If there are more than six, you will almost certainly find that they are not strategic enough.

Figure 10.2 shows three annual planning away days in the last three months of the year followed by the launch to the business in January. Each monthly strategic meeting will then review and adjust the plans where necessary. Each quarter, one of the monthly strategic meetings should be replaced by a slightly longer off-site meeting (these are often done every six months in smaller organizations). The quarterly off-site

**Figure 10.2: Annual meeting, planning and
communications calendar**

meeting will look at broader external themes such as changes in the industry, new competitors, the economic climate and new regulations, as well as looking internally at your people (rising stars and poor performers), new strategic priorities, development of the top team, possible acquisitions and interest from acquirers (although this is likely to be done immediately).

Engaging your people

When an organization creates its strategic priorities and communicates them to the business, it can feel like a torrent of information delivered to the employees. The danger is that people will just switch off after the first few presentations. Two actions are essential at this time. The first is to engage your people in meaningful discussions around the strategic priorities and the second is to provide a focus for the next period of the year.

1. *Engagement in strategic priorities.* Put your strategic priorities in context. Never miss an opportunity to remind people of your decision filters: purpose, vision, values and strategy. Just like when you were at school, make sure you include the working out, not just the answer! Make sure you include all relevant context behind your strategic priorities or people will make it up themselves (and they might not arrive at the right answer). If you are launching a new product – why? If you are going into a new market – why? If you creating a new department – why? If you have developed a new brand – why? Don't just give your

people the answer, give them the reasons too. Once you've given them the context, ask your people relevant and meaningful questions about what they need to do to deliver in their part of the business. This will create buy-in and ownership.

2. *A thematic goal or focus for your business.* When you have created your strategic priorities for the following year, a discussion should follow in your SLT about launching the plans to the business. You want to excite and energize your people, not drown them with too much information. You must decide as a top team what your thematic goal or 'rallying cry' is. This is one key theme that can apply across your business for a period of time. It should be clearly laid out, and needs to be seen as critical to business success. This is not saying that all your plans are not important; rather, the point is to get your people focused and energized about one element of your plan at a time – such as a new product launch. To do this, your marketing team would have a plan for the launch, the sales team would also have a plan to sell, operations would be involved in planning how to deliver and customer service and account management would have plans once it was launched to market. The product launch becomes your thematic goal. You would develop an internal communications campaign about all aspects of the product launch and before getting to the end of that campaign your SLT would start thinking about the next thematic goal.

Plan your strategic priorities

Questions for you and your leadership team

1. Do you have a clear set of strategic priorities for the year, broken down by quarters?
2. Do you have clear measures, targets and timescales with a manager accountable to deliver each strategic priority?
3. Do you have an annual planning process that facilitates the creation of your strategic priorities?
4. How well do all your departmental plans feed into your strategic priorities?
5. How well do you use your decision filters (Chapters 1–4) to guide the creation of your strategic priorities?

Chapter 11

Measure your success

If you only look at financial performance, you are only seeing what's showing up in the rear-view mirror.

Introduction

To measure your success, you must start by answering the question, 'What does success look like for your business?' Every industry is different and within each industry every business will be different. If you don't think your business is different, then go back to Chapter 4 and work out how to create competitive advantage. What you need to understand is what your critical numbers are, and these will flow out of your vision and your strategy – in other words, what you want to become **and** what makes you different. Part of the strategy model is what your economic engine is i.e. how you make money. When you truly understand your competitive advantage, it will be easier to come up with your critical numbers.

Deciding on your Key Performance Indicators

When deciding what Key Performance Indicators (KPIs) are important to your business, there are a number of principles you need to consider:

1. *Useful, not just interesting.* One of the dangers of KPIs is that they can be really interesting to know, but you must make a choice and only choose those that provide really useful information, which allows you to make critical decisions.

2. *Not too many and not too few.* Remember these are not just performance indicators, they are Key Performance Indicators – in other words, those that are vital to know and track. To land on what is key in your business might take a few attempts, but in the end you must be clear that the few you are tracking tell you exactly how your business is doing. Most businesses with which I work have 10–15 KPIs that they look at regularly at a leadership team level.

3. *Increased knowledge and understanding.* People are not stupid, but sometimes business leaders believe that the numbers won't be understood in parts of the business, 'so there's no point in telling them'. It is simply not true: numbers can really educate people so they understand that their actions reduce costs, thereby increasing profits and allowing more to be spent on bonuses or investments in the business. This doesn't mean, however, that every person needs every number – too many that aren't relevant will just be confusing.

4. *Transparency, empowerment and ownership.* People need to know which numbers their actions can influence. But numbers must not just be given to people. The difference is huge between giving someone a number and asking them to hit it and asking someone

what numbers they believe they should have, that they can truly influence. When someone sets their own measures and targets, they own them. When people can see the link, their motivation increases as they watch the effects their actions have on the numbers.

5. *Driving internal competitiveness and changing behaviour.* In a business with which I have been working, the CEO has told me how each of his regions is shown not only their sales numbers, but also all the numbers for the other regions. Once a site has achieved over an agreed baseline (which means it has reached a certain minimum level of profit), the staff receive a percentage of the profits. When staff in one region see that another region is receiving a bonus, they ask their manager what they need to do differently to get a bonus. The managers can then discuss with staff the targets they need to hit to trigger the bonus. Staff are now informed, and are owning and driving their own actions to impact the numbers and ultimately their own bonuses.

6. *They are balanced.* Measures need to be financial and non-financial, and need to be looked at in terms of telling a story of the past (lag) as well as predicting what the story might be in the future (lead). For example, a monthly sales figure tells you what you sold last month, but it doesn't tell you what you will sell next month. Certainly, if there is a trend over a long period of time then it is a good guide, but you will need other measures to give you reassurance about the future – for example, number of client meetings

in the last month or number of pitches coupled with your pitch conversion rates. Put all these together and you have both lag and lead indicators, and thus a good idea about how you are likely to perform next month. Non-financial measures must reflect all major parts of your business – for example, sales, marketing, people, operations and customer experience.

Financial horses for courses: We are not all the same

Financial numbers are the obvious ones measured by all businesses – that is, total revenue (sales), gross profit, net profit (after costs are taken out) and cash. However, despite being the platform that every business needs, financial metrics should only make up part of your measurement. What you must decide (based on your vision and strategy) is how important revenue, cash and profit are to you. Let me explain. I work with some fast-growth software businesses, which have investors with a long-term horizon. The CEO has spent years following a strategy to invest the owners' (shareholders') money in R&D and marketing, without ever making a profit. The vision is to take the business to a certain size, when the profits will kick in and the value of the business will be significant. Organically grown businesses (with no outside investors) need to make profit and have larger cash reserves, on which they can fall back if times get tough. Some organizations with which I work have a wind-up cash position. This is a figure that will cover the business if they have to close in six months' time, pay their staff and pay off all their debts. It provides their safety net.

Let's look at some very different businesses in different industries to see what I mean.

IKEA

In Chapter 2, we saw that IKEA's vision is 'A better everyday life for the many people'. We also looked at IKEA's strategy in Chapter 4. The company's competitive advantage is centred around three things:

- limited customer service (few sales staff and self-transport)
- low manufacturing costs (ample on-site inventory)
- modular furniture design (in-house design and ease of assembly).

From this very clear point of difference, we can see what IKEA's critical numbers are likely to be. There will probably be something about the ratio of customer service staff to customers (which should be low); there will be a number related to the cost of manufacturing as a percentage of sales revenues; there will be a percentage of revenues invested into R&D (in order to produce modular self-assembly furniture at a low price to customers). IKEA's vision provides real focus about who the company's customers will be: 'the many people'. This isn't for the few who are very wealthy, although you'll still find a few of them buying for their student children at university; IKEA is for everyone at some time point in their lives. I don't know of anyone who hasn't shopped at IKEA.

Kelly's Storage

Kelly's Storage is a dynamic and forward-thinking storage company in Guildford in the United Kingdom. Its business is mobile storage and document storage, and it has acquired several synergistic companies over the years to strengthen its customer offerings and add to the Kelly's family. Two years ago, CEO Paul Martin decided that he wanted to be transparent with Kelly's key financial metrics with the aim of everyone in the business acting like owners and being accountable for their own numbers. This idea came from Jack Stack's book *The Great Game of Business*.[1] Kelly's wanted everyone, no matter where they worked in the business, to own up to three targets that they could influence. Hitting their own targets would contribute to quarterly bonuses for everyone, no matter where they were in the business: if the numbers were hit, everyone from driver to director would get the same amount of money.

I spent a fascinating hour sitting in on one of Kelly's end-of-month meetings, where everyone reported their numbers and saw how everyone else was doing. The engagement was terrific and so was the commitment to reaching or beating targets. Light-hearted discussion was commonplace about how everyone was doing and how they could improve.

---

[1] Jack Stack, *The Great Game of Business: The Only Sensible Way to Run a Company*, 2013.

I also witnessed peer-to-peer accountability where everyone wanted to pull their weight and not let anyone else down. Paul's mantra is that if you don't know the score, you can't affect the game.

However you decide your business should be run, it is clear to me that the more your people are engaged in owning their numbers, the more they want to hit them and show others in the business how they are doing. KPIs through a business must be joined up from top to bottom. Figure 11.1 shows the three broad areas to address in a business.

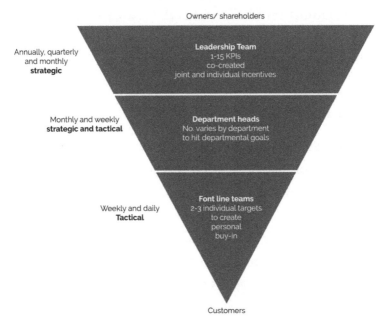

Figure 11.1: Business KPIs and targets inverted triangle

At the leadership level, you'll want 10 to 15 KPIs so that your dashboard will give you a realistic picture of how the business is running. You should be able to pick two or three that are the most crucial, related to your strategy. These should all be co-created with your leadership team so that everyone will support everyone else towards the delivery of your overall business goals. These will be monitored at monthly strategic meetings and quarterly off-sites, and reset annually.

Departmental heads will then set more granular KPIs for their departments that allow them to hit the more strategic leadership-level KPIs. These will be monitored monthly and at weekly tactical meetings.

On the front line, everyone should contribute to the setting of their own KPIs so that they have two to three that they can influence every day. These are monitored during daily huddle meetings and weekly tactical meetings.

Creating a balanced set of KPIs

Finally, let's look in a bit more detail at what 'balanced' means for a business. It was Robert S. Kaplan and David P. Norton who first popularized the 'balanced scorecard' approach with their 1992 article in the *Harvard Business Review* entitled 'Measures That Drive Performance', followed by their 1996 book, *Balanced Scorecard: Translating Strategy into Action*.[2] The important message is not to rely only on financial data to inform your leadership team about how your business is doing.

The following are the main areas that we need to measure (with examples of some of the key metrics under each):

---

[2] Robert S. Kaplan and David P. Norton, *Balanced Scorecard: Translating Strategy into Action*, 1996.

1. Financial:
   - sales revenue
   - revenue growth
   - gross profit
   - net profit
   - EBIT and EBITDA (earnings before interest and tax, depreciation and amortization)
   - total assets
   - total costs
   - costs of goods sold (costs of materials and labour used to produce a product)
   - operating cash flow (amount of cash generated by regular business operations)
   - debtor days (how quickly cash owed to you is being collected from debtors)
   - creditor days (how quickly we settle our bills with our suppliers)
   - accounts receivable (the money we are owed by our customers)
   - accounts payable (the money we owe to suppliers)
   - wind-up cash position (the cash in the bank we would need to wind up the business if we had to in a given timeframe).

2. Customers:
   - customer experience (e.g. net promoter score)
   - number of customers
   - total customer tickets vs. number of open tickets
   - average resolution time of customer tickets
   - customer retention

- average revenue and profit per customer
- percentage of sales from top two customers (this can vary)
- number of existing vs. new customers
- customer churn.

3. Sales and marketing:
   a. General:
      - sales closed per sales rep
      - cost per customer acquisition
      - product and service mix sold to each customer
      - total pipeline value per rep
      - lead conversion rates (how many leads are converted)
      - referrals
      - ROI on advertising spend.

   b. Digital marketing:
      - social (followers, engagement, site visits, conversions)
      - search engine optimization (SEO – impressions, site visits, conversions, revenue)
      - pay per click (PPC – impressions, click-through rate, conversions, cost per acquisition)
      - email (delivery rate, open rate, click-through rate and conversion rate)
      - content – for example, videos, webinars, podcasts, blogs and vlogs, newsletters (views, visits, bounce rate, content shares and conversions).

c. Subscription model:
    - monthly unique visitors
    - trial sign ups
    - trial pay up rates
    - monthly paying subscribers.

4. People:
    - engagement (e.g. Gallup Q12)
    - average cost per employee
    - average cost of recruitment
    - training and development days per employee
    - training and development days as percentage of revenue or profit
    - number of employee suggestions
    - staff churn
    - sick leave per year
    - staff capability profile (e.g. number of BTECs, degrees, PhDs, etc.)
    - overtime hours.

5. Operations:
    - percentage of on-time delivery
    - transportation costs
    - average delivery time (hours, minutes)
    - defect rates
    - inventory
    - process cycle time
    - utilization (e.g. people, machines, transport, etc.)
    - R&D as percentage of revenue or profit
    - return on innovation investment.

Once you've agreed on a set of KPIs, find a way to automate them across your business so that you get the data you need when you need it. Too many manual systems are unreliable and will do you more harm than good in the long run. There are many financial business intelligence tools and dashboards that can support you in tracking KPIs automatically once you have taken the time to set them up properly.

Measure your success

Questions for you and your leadership team

1. Do the numbers (KPIs) that you monitor support the delivery of your strategy?
2. Do you have a balanced (lag, lead, financial and non-financial) set of KPIs for your business?
3. Are your KPIs monitored and evaluated monthly, with actions taken when you are off track?
4. Do your department heads have a set of KPIs that feed into the overall KPIs for the business?
5. Do your people at every level of your business have two to three measures and targets that they own and can influence, and they can be rewarded on if they reach their targets?

Chapter 12

Execute through great meetings

Your meetings should be the best part of your day.

Introduction

Gordon Ramsay, one of the world's most famous Michelin-starred chefs, has said that you can tell the quality of a great restaurant by how good the bread rolls are. In a business, the same goes for meetings. Meetings should be the best part of the day; they are where you get things agreed, where deep discussions take place on the important issues, where you can show support and care for your colleagues, where you can challenge them on how things are going and ultimately where your strategy gets delivered.

Meetings require discipline, planning, good timekeeping, great facilitation and chairing, the right people in the room, energy, passion, tension, care, commitment, accountability and praise! It's not surprising, with such a list, that most meetings just don't live up to expectations. In this chapter, I will unpack the types of meetings you should have, how often you should have them and how to make them the best part of your day.

Types of meetings

Meetings broadly fall into two categories: strategic and tactical. The first rule is not to mix them in the same meeting. There are some good reasons why. First, your brain finds it difficult to be big picture one minute and small detail the next; also, meetings generally fall into the two camps anyway. They are either strategic or tactical.

Let's start with the short, daily, tactical meetings and work our way up to the quarterly full-day strategic ones.

The daily huddle

The daily huddle is something that happens in teams, big and small, in all parts of an organization. Its purpose is to share what is going on in a team that day – to say quickly what everyone is doing that day, highlight upcoming challenges and opportunities and get back to work. Deeper discussions are then taken offline after the meeting, so not to waste the time of anyone who doesn't need to be involved in the discussion. They are quick, with each person providing a maximum two-minute input (which should be timed by someone in the team), and they need to have high energy and be kept fast paced. Let me outline an example of how they work. A daily huddle takes place and you find out that Jim, one of your colleagues, has a key client meeting that afternoon off-site. This means that (1) the rest of the team knows where Jim is that afternoon; (2) the team can provide support as needed; and (3) they can wish him good luck for the meeting. This was all shared in two minutes in the daily huddle. If this had not taken place, then team members might be left asking where Jim was, as they might have hoped for a meeting themselves, and there would be a lost opportunity to provide both practical and emotional support for his meeting. In the daily tactical meeting, you don't get into any of the deep issues – those are taken offline afterwards with the individual, and the two-minute rule keeps the meeting lively and engaging.

The weekly tactical meeting

This meeting usually takes place on a Friday. It's a team meeting that happens in all teams across the organization. It takes a little longer than the daily huddle – usually a maximum of 30–45 minutes – and has several objectives:

- *From the team leader:* summarizing how the week has gone, highlighting successes and challenges, giving praise where praise is due, showing progress against the monthly objectives and targets, looking ahead to the next week and sharing an overview of what it looks like.
- *From the team:* highlights and challenges for each of them, individual learning, thoughts on the week ahead.

The leader should ensure that everyone in the team is encouraged to provide input into the discussions. Don't let the 'nodding dogs' syndrome occur. As the leader, you want to know what is on people's minds and where they need to be challenged, as well as supported. As Patrick Lencioni states in his books, 'Leaders mine for conflict'.

The monthly strategic meeting

This is when your senior leadership team comes together to share where you are against your annual strategic priorities. Your agenda is pre-set by the timetable to which you are working, to deliver the plans and actions that sit behind each of your strategic priorities.

Figure 12.1 shows an example of six strategic priorities for a year, spread over 12 months. Some are starting mid-year because there are previous strategic priorities wrapping around from the previous year.

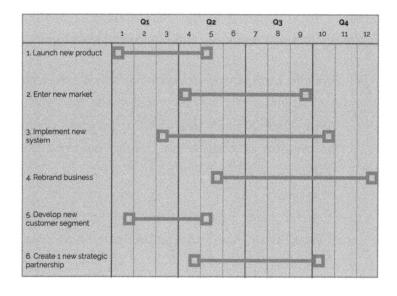

**Figure 12.1: Strategic priorities over
a year – simplified table**

Each of these headline priorities will have a detailed plan behind it. As you can see, you can pick a month in the year

– for example, month 4 – and see where you should be on the six priorities:

1. Launch new product should be in the last phase.
2. Enter new market has just started.
3. Implement new system is a couple of months in.
4. Rebrand our business has not yet started, but a previous priority will be coming to completion (from the previous year).
5. Develop new customer segment is in the last phase.
6. Create new partnership is just about to kick off.

It is easy to see what should be on the agenda now. Each of these priorities will have one (and only one) person accountable in the senior leadership team.

Remember, if there is more than one person accountable, then no one is accountable.

There should be clear targets and measures for each strategic priority and based on the actions agreed at the previous monthly strategic meeting, it will be clear to all what should have been achieved by then.

When going through each of the strategic priorities, the most time should be spent on those that are *not on track*. Many businesses operate a RAG (red, amber and green) traffic light system. The senior leadership team can then see graphically where you are against each strategic priority and focus on those that need to be challenged and supported. Those that are showing green can then be discussed only briefly and the focus of the meeting can be on amber and particularly red priorities.

The urgent strategic meeting

There are going to be times during the year when something important and urgent happens mid-month. An opportunity arises to go into a new market or pitch at short notice for a big project, or a business approaches you wanting to discuss buying or merging with you. It is vital that these opportunities are discussed and agreed by the senior leadership team. They may be able to wait for the next meeting, but they may not – in which case, the team may need to come together mid-month to discuss the issues and decide on a course of action. This, of course, will create an issue for the business that is sometimes ignored, leaving the same people just trying to fit in more work. When you add another strategic priority, then something usually needs to change: more or different resources, training and development requirements, new partners and so on. The issue is how to decide whether or not to go for a new opportunity. That brings us to the in-year strategic opportunity.

In the late 1990s, I was working as a consultant delivering change programmes into Toyota and Lexus. I was asked to put together a proposal for a staff conference. This was a new strategic opportunity on top of what Toyota were already committed to delivering. It would require additional resources: time, people, money and a great deal of commitment from the business. I was asked to put forward a return on investment (ROI) for the programme and, along with the

HR director, to present it to the board for approval. Toyota is simply wonderful at process; it calls this an A3 (because that is the size of the paper it is written on). Toyota provided a structure of the areas that needed to be included in the ROI. I prepared it and presented it to the board, and after much discussion and challenge it was approved. New resources were allocated, we shared together how important this would be for the business and we got on with it.

This approach to dealing with in-year strategic opportunities needs to be adapted to your business. Here is a list of the key questions you need to put into any process you decide to use:

1. What is the problem or opportunity we are trying to overcome or promote?
2. What is the goal we want to achieve?
3. What are the key actions that we will need to take?
4. How long will this take?
5. What is your idea or solution?
6. What are the expected benefits for our business?
7. How will you measure success (key measures and targets)?
8. What investment is required in terms of resources, time, people, effort, etc.?
9. How does it fit with our decision filters (our purpose, vision, strategy and values)?

Producing an easy-to-use form for people to access when they have a new idea will be hugely beneficial to your business, not only by creating a standardized way of assessing ideas, but also by forcing people at every level to think like business owners.

The quarterly off-site meeting (retreat)

The quarterly off-site meeting is the most strategic of all your meetings, and will reap real benefits for you and your top team. This is one of your meetings that should be run by an external facilitator so that everyone can participate without the distraction of running the session. It is impossible to facilitate and take part effectively at the same time.

The purpose of this meeting is to step back from the business and look at the bigger picture. Below are listed the areas that should be covered in this off-site meeting. For the first two questions, you should consider using SWOT and PESTLE strategic analysis tools (as described in Chapter 4).

- How are we doing so far this year? Are we on track against our strategic priorities and KPIs? What are the key challenges we need to solve? What are the key opportunities we should take advantage of?
- How has the external environment changed?
- How is our SLT performing? Are we all performing and hitting our individual KPIs? Are we all motivated and fulfilled in our roles? Is further training and development required or is individual coaching or mentoring needed for key people? You should consider a 360 open feedback session here.
- How are the key people in our business performing? How are our A players doing and do we have a plan to

keep them and keep them motivated? How are our C players performing? Do we have a plan to move them into B or A players or move them out of the business?

- *Team development.* These off-sites are a great opportunity to continue to build the effectiveness of the team. See Chapter 6 for further information on what to do. In broad terms, you will be looking at new skills development as well as deepening your understanding of each member of the team and building trust.

The all-hands or town hall meeting

This is a regular meeting to engage the whole business in what has happened and what the plan is going forward. It should not be a one-way communication meeting full of PowerPoint slides and talks from the senior leadership team. It should have a theme and it must engage. It should be welcomed by your people. These meetings provide a great opportunity to find out what is on everyone's mind and to seek new ideas. The frequency of this meeting varies by organization. Some businesses with which I have worked do one every month and some do one every quarter. They are usually one to two hours long and contain a mixture of the following:

- an overview of business progress
- an update on success of major initiatives and projects
- new products and services, markets, clients, partners
- stories of successes and occasions where things didn't go so well; this provides an opportunity for leadership to

show vulnerability, to admit when they made the wrong call (for the right reasons) and to discuss what to do

- feedback on staff surveys with actions on what improvements will be made.

Annual business planning meetings

See Chapter 10 for information about these meetings.

The 121 meeting

This final meeting is, of course, perhaps the most important and, in many organizations, the least well done. The old-style annual appraisal meeting is defunct and gone. When you strip back the purpose of a 121 meeting between two people, it is ultimately about one person knowing how they are doing. It should be done formally every month and informally every week. The weekly meeting is a catch-up and feedback session. It's intended to make sure you are both on the same page and that praise is given as well as areas to improve discussed and agreed. The more formal monthly meeting should follow a structure and be formally recorded so that anyone (who is allowed) can see how the person is performing. One of the problems that can develop is if a person's performance starts to dip over time, but nothing has been formally recorded. It is then one person's word against another. There are three areas that should be covered in a monthly 121 meeting:

1. performance against objectives and targets
2. development of personal mastery (see motivation in Chapter 7) – everyone should be developing

themselves through training and development of one kind or another every month, which could be formal courses and training, books and TED Talks and/or coaching and mentoring

3. living the organizational values, which need to be discussed regularly if they are to be embedded in the organization. A discussion should be had at every monthly 121 to see how the individual is living the values in their everyday work.

Running great meetings

The aim of every meeting is to make it engaging, impactful and action oriented. This can be done by sticking to certain standards and approaches. Great meetings, like great presentations, follow a similar flow. They have a powerful start that instantly engages you, they have drama and tension when you discuss the key issues of the day and they have a great ending that wraps up the meeting with actions, accountabilities and what ongoing communication is required.

The agenda

The agenda must be pre-set and take input from those who need to be present. It should broadly follow the principles of the most important areas (which often take the longest time) coming first and not last, as many meetings seem to adopt. Different people should be asked to take responsibility for different parts of the agenda and each element should be timed. The agenda should be issued well in advance of the meeting so people can prepare properly.

Energy, tempo and timing

The first few minutes will set the energy levels and tempo of the meeting. If you want a high-energy, engaging meeting, then it must start that way and the leader or chair/facilitator needs to set the tone. I always start meetings standing up unless there are only a couple of people in the meeting. I decide before I kick off the meeting what my intention is. If the meeting has several parts, then the intention will shift as the meeting progresses. At the outset, I might want to show positivity and high energy, and I might want to begin with a story that will bring to life a point I want to make. As the meeting progresses, I might shift to actions and accountabilities for everyone. Meetings must always start and end on time. If some people are not there, start anyway – they must apologize to the group and explain why they believe their time is more important than that of everyone else in the room. If that happens, they are unlikely to show up late again, but if you allow the meeting to wait until they arrive, you can guarantee that they will turn up late again. Starting a meeting late erodes your credibility as a leader.

A great way of showing everyone the cost of a meeting is to use a meeting calculator.[1] By entering in the number of people, average salaries and length of the meeting, they will calculate how much the meeting is costing you. When you multiply that by the number of these meetings you hold in a year, you can often come up with quite a sobering figure. A

---

[1] 'Estimate the cost of a meeting with this calculator', *Harvard Business Review*, January 2016, https://hbr.org/2016/01/estimate-the-cost-of-a-meeting-with-this-calculator.

note of caution: some organizations run meetings that start and end on the hour. This means that if you are in back-to-back meetings, you'll automatically be late for the next one. One organization I worked with always ended its meetings at 10 minutes to the hour – that way you won't be late.

The check-in

A great way to start a meeting is to use the check-in. There are numerous ways to do this and it can be a good idea to vary the way you do it slightly in order to keep it fresh. Let me share one version with you that you can adapt to your organization's culture.

Starting with the leader in the room, everyone, one at a time, gives their score for that day/week/month (depending on the meeting frequency) for business, personal and health and wellbeing, out of 10. When you start off, you may just start with business scores, but as people get used to this process, you can add the other categories. Give people a time limit. I usually give people two minutes each and have someone in the room responsible for time-keeping. People then give their scores and a narrative around them. Scores are a great way of getting into challenges and issues. Say someone gives a score of 6 for business, they have to say why it is so low, how the group could help them to get it to a 9 or 10, what support they need. Likewise for personal, and health and wellbeing. These two latter categories show you care about the whole person.

The check-in also allows people to open up about what is troubling them. The more you run this sort of check-in, the more people will feel comfortable about opening up. Sometimes it will give you an opportunity to take something offline afterwards.

In addition to asking for a narrative around the scores, you can also vary a question each month, depending on what is important or what you specifically want to raise. For example:

- What's the one big thing on your mind?
- What's the biggest opportunity you have?
- What's the 'elephant in the room'?
- Who is the person/department needing the most support?
- Who is the person/department doing the best job?

Updates

Depending on the type of meeting, there will be updates to provide to people about how things are progressing. Any actions from the last meeting can be shared before the meeting starts by email or can be discussed in the meeting if required.

The issue/opportunity/challenge

Perhaps the most important purpose of monthly meetings is to get into the key issues the organization is facing and to get your most able people involved in those discussions. It is not always a good idea just to have side meetings to discuss and solve issues. The senior leadership team is there to support and challenge all areas of the business to deliver on their plans. It is often the director or manager who isn't involved day to day in an area who asks the best questions and comes up with the best ideas.

Actions, accountabilities and timescales

Meetings must always include the actions that have been decided, who will take the action and when it will be completed by (only one person accountable for each action point and it is they who should report back). Let the person accountable set the timescales and agree them in the meeting. If the leader of the team imposes a timescale on someone else, then they will not own it.

✳ ✳ ✳

Roles

Multiple roles can be allocated in a meeting. The most important is the chair or facilitator. Do not assume that if you are the most senior person in the room you must be the facilitator of the meeting. It can help enormously to have someone who is skilled at facilitation running the meeting so that the team leader can focus on getting the agenda points covered and actions agreed. After some practice, it can work very well as a double act. Another important role is as a time-keeper – again, it can be useful to give this role to someone who is good at it and who has no problems interrupting conversations to get the meeting back on track. The third role is the note-taker; this can be occupied by the same person or rotated. Another role is values and standards monitor, and this can also be rotated. This important role is there to make sure that the values, standards and/or teamship rules are upheld. Roles engage people in the meeting and can keep a meeting running on time, with good notes and actions as well as reinforcing the company's values.

Personality types in meetings

Numerous psychometric profiling tools can be used in organizations to help us understand ourselves and our colleagues. Belbin Teams Profiles are great for a whole team to see where their strengths and 'allowable weaknesses' are and what might be missing from the team. Individual profiling can be achieved through many tools. The most popular ones in use today are the Myers Briggs Personality Types (MBTI) and DISC profiling. The simplest is DISC profiling, which has evolved into a number of versions.

There are four main personality types in DISC profiling that we all have. These are particularly important to consider when running or being in a meeting. These four types are often referred to in different ways, but they all stem from the initial work by undertaken by William Moulton Marston at Harvard. His 1928 book, *Emotions of Normal People,*[2] explains his theories. These theories eventually became the profiling system known as DISC, which is an acronym standing for Dominance, Influence, Steadiness and Conscientiousness. The most useful and memorable version of this is the version developed by Merrick Rosenberg, whose book, *Taking Flight,* turns each of the four areas into a different bird (Figure 12.2).

---

[2] William Moulton Marston, *Emotions of Normal People*, 1928.

Figure 12.2: Taking flight with DISC

The beauty of this version is that it is so memorable. I can always remember that I am mainly Owl, with secondary tendencies of Dove and Eagle. It is also very easy to see what they are. The Eagle is the dominant one (it rules the sky). The Parrot is the expressive, colourful and talkative one. Doves like a harmonious environment. Owls look for detail and accuracy, and they don't seek the spotlight. Let's look at them in more detail – particularly how they show up in meetings and how to manage the four types.

The first thing to notice is that Eagles and Parrots are extroverts. This means that they think out loud while they are considering their point of view. In contrast, Owls and Doves are introverts, who think through their arguments before presenting them to the group. This immediately creates the issue that without proper 'bird management', the Eagles and Parrots will tend to dominate any meeting. Both Eagles and Parrots therefore work best when there is a timed agenda. They must be heard, but not allowed to take up all the airtime. Owls and Doves need the agenda in advance as they then have time to think things through before the meeting.

I was chairing a meeting of executives a few years ago and we were helping one of them with a thorny issue. The group had a cross-section of introverts and extroverts in the room. After we had questioned the executive in the hot seat and agreed what the key issue was, we started on a round of ideas and observations from each person. I started with 'John', who was the executive to my left – he was a very bright man, a Cambridge University graduate who ran the biggest business around the table. He had very little to say, which I found strange. We went around the room and everyone put their points across. I was confused at first until I remembered that John was an Owl and therefore an introvert. I hadn't given him time to think. The next issue that we ran, I asked who would like to go first. The Parrots jumped in first, followed by the Eagles, then came the Doves and lastly the Owls. This allowed the introverts to think through their points before voicing them. It gave everyone equal airtime. Everyone played to their bird type. The Eagles were strategic and convinced of their ideas, the Parrots made a few jokes during their ideas, they talked over their time and were full of ideas, jumping from one to another. The Owls were detailed and analytical, quoting books and TED Talks, and gave lots of details about what they thought needed to be done. Finally, the Doves talked about the effect of the decision on the people and how they would feel about the outcome.

When you think about this story, you can see how powerful it is to have a mixture of personality types in your team and you can also see how they must be managed in different ways. There is also a self-check that the extroverts (Eagles and Parrots) can use. Ask them to consider whether they are speaking too much – are they involving the introverts and really listening to what they have to say? The introverts also have a self-check – are they expressing themselves and really saying what they are thinking?

Execute through great meetings

Questions for you and your leadership team

1. Do you have a meeting rhythm in your business from strategic to tactical that is adhered to?
2. Do your meetings monitor and assess progress against your strategic or tactical (depending on the meeting) priorities and then create actions to get you back on track where necessary?
3. Are your meetings engaging, informative and challenging, with clear outcomes and accountabilities?

4. Do your people understand different personality types and adjust their behaviour to get the best out of others?

5. Are your meetings well planned (with clear agendas) and facilitated?

Summary of Part 3

So there you have the third part of *The Leadership Map* – executing your strategy. Somebody once asked me whether it was better to have a good strategy badly executed or a bad strategy well executed. I would say that the former leaves you hugely frustrated that you are not getting the results you think you deserve and the latter probably puts you out of business. Of course, you need both: a great strategy superbly executed. When you think of the three parts of *The Leadership Map*, they require very different skills. Some of us are great at seeing the big picture, imagining the future, engaging and inspiring people, while others are great at building teams and developing people and yet others are brilliant at developing and executing on detailed plans and running great meetings. It's unlikely that you are going to be good at everything. It's more likely that you are naturally better at one of the three parts of this book. This doesn't mean that you can't improve in the other areas, but it's difficult and unusual to be brilliant at all three. That's why I've provided the questions at the end of each chapter – so you can see where your strengths currently lie and address them. The key to great leaders is that they surround themselves with people who are better than them at the things they are not so good at.

Now the hard bit: go and implement the things you have learned. You'll make some mistakes along the way (that's to be expected, and remember that's how you learn and grow), you'll be challenged on the things you say and the things you do, but say them and do them anyway. Becoming a great leader is hard, but as my dad used to say to me, if it's worth doing, it's worth doing well. Good luck in your journey!

PART 4
Conclusion

Chapter 13

The map

Iwrote *The Leadership Map* with the intention of providing leaders with a blueprint to run a business. Leaders, as well as aspiring leaders, can read the 12 chapters in this book and discover what they need to do, as well as reflect on how they are currently showing up. The 12 areas contained in *The Leadership Map* should not be taken individually, according to taste. A bit like a set of values in an organization, leaders need to understand all the elements of the map really well – they can't pick and choose, and they must then decide where to focus their energies. You will find that you are naturally more interested in some areas than others, that some areas are in your comfort zone and some are not and that you are rather good at some and less so at others. The best leaders bring great people in to complement them in the areas where they are not going to focus. In my experience of working with numerous successful businesses, both small SMEs and large global corporates, these 12 areas are the essential elements that successful leaders and leadership teams do exceptionally well.

The first four areas of the map must be in place so that everything else can work – they provide the platform for your business. They require a huge amount of strategic thinking, they take time and emotional energy and they are not simple. However, they are essential to provide complete clarity and alignment in your top team and for everyone else in the organization. With this platform in place, you will know:

- why you exist (your purpose) (Chapter 1)
- where you want to go (your unreasonable dream or vision) (Chapter 2)
- how you will behave (your values) (Chapter 3)
- what your competitive advantage is (your strategy) (Chapter 4).

When these are crystal clear, decision-making is far simpler – not just for the board and senior leadership team, but for your front-line workers. So you must start there.

You can only achieve your unreasonable dream, or vision, through your people and through supporting structures and processes. Part 2 started with Chapter 5, on challenging the status quo; creating a culture of challenge, stretch, creativity and support, underpinned by standardized processes that support open loop thinking along with constant learning and growth. Chapter 6 then showed you how to create your dream team. A top team with strategic decision filters in place will achieve nothing if its members are not working in a cohesive fashion and do not demand excellence from each other every day. Chapter 7 allowed us to step into culture and explore motivation, engagement and happiness – three areas vital to creating a workforce that will willingly show up and give their all, every day. Finally, Chapter 8 discussed something leaders need in abundance: grit or resilience. Grit is something that we developed through childhood, through the experiences that shaped us, added to by the challenges we have faced throughout adulthood. We must also understand how to recruit for grit and develop it further in ourselves and in our people.

Part 3 concluded *The Leadership Map* by discussing strategy execution. Our strategic decision filters are in place and our people are on board, and they are skilfully putting everything into their roles with fortitude and resilience. Finally, we need structures and processes to help us to deliver. Part 3 began in Chapter 9 with a look at organizational structure – something that, as leaders, we rarely examine. With the wrong structure in place, silos can quickly develop and the opportunity for empowerment and accountability can be lost. We must find and assemble a structure that supports our strategy. We also need a robust annual process to create a brilliant set of strategic priorities, discussed in Chapter 10. These are underpinned by a scorecard of KPIs (Chapter 11), delivered through high energy, challenging and supportive meetings (Chapter 12), from the monthly strategic meeting at the top to the daily huddle in our teams.

If you take the time and energy to put all these elements in place in your business, you will have given yourself the best chance of success. Leading and managing teams and businesses is hard: you need to learn and grow every day and try things – some of which will succeed and some of which will not. Regroup and go again.

For more inspiration and help, go to my website and sign up to my newsletter, listen to my podcast, read my blog or apply for The Leadership Map open programme. And finally, good luck!

About the author

Ian Windle is an award-winning leadership speaker, executive coach and team excellence builder.

In 2018 he delivered a TEDx Talk entitled 'Why Everyone Needs an Unreasonable Dream'. He regularly speaks at conferences in the United Kingdom and internationally, and works with leadership teams on their strategy, vision and values, as well as on developing their capabilities to perform at their peak.

Ian is also a Vistage Group Chair, coaching and developing groups of CEOs and key executives in Surrey, England to fulfil their individual potential, create balanced lives and grow their businesses.

Ian's first career was in the Foreign and Commonwealth Office, working in many European capitals and in South-East Asia. In 1996 he moved into consultancy with Celemi International, where for 10 years he was Managing Director of the company's UK business.

He has an MBA from Henley Business School, is a Chartered Member of the Institute of Personnel and Development, has an Executive and Corporate Coach Diploma (ILM7) and a Diploma in Marketing and is an Accredited Belbin Team Roles Facilitator.

Ian lives in Surrey, England with his wife Jacqueline and their twin daughters.

Website: https://ianwindle.com

Monthly Blogs: https://ianwindle.com/blog

The Gritty Leaders Club Podcast:
https://ianwindle.com/podcasts

Monthly Newsletter: https://ianwindle.com

The Leadership Map, two-year open programme:
https://ianwindle.com/theleadershipmap

Acknowledgements

It has been a fascinating journey putting this book together. The good news was that I started with a lot of content from the Leadership Map programme that I had been running for two years. What I hadn't realized is how much richer my programme would become because of all the subsequent research I would do when writing the book. At times it has felt totally indulgent, being allowed to research all these topics that I love, to add to my own learning and growth, and then being able to share it through the pages of the book. At other times, when I spent long evenings or weekends writing and researching, I felt totally selfish, eating up time I knew I should be spending with my family. I am sure that, like most authors, I don't feel fully satisfied with my work – especially as this is what I know today, now, and that will change tomorrow. Having said that, I do feel proud of this book as it stands, and I hope it will help you on your leadership journey (as there definitely is no destination!).

Family

When my twin girls were five and I had a good steady job as the MD of a business local to my home, I asked my wife whether she'd be happy if I left to start my own business. She was as encouraging then as she was about the idea of writing my book. Both were untried, stretching and a little bit selfish, and both have allowed me to stretch and grow on the way to fulfil my purpose of 'inspiring leadership'.

So my first acknowledgement must be to my wife and children. I could have spent more time being with you at weekends and evenings, but you would have had a less fulfilled husband and father, one who had not tried to reach his full potential.

Mentors, coaches and peer group

I've been so lucky during the last eight and a half years to be part of the Vistage community. I'm surrounded by exceptional leaders, who have chosen to devote considerable parts of their lives to being Vistage Group Chairs. They have inspired me, coached me and challenged me to keep pushing and developing myself to become a better version tomorrow of the person I am today. The book was merely the next stepping-stone along the journey.

Clients and other contributors

Since 2006, when I started my own business, my job has never felt like work. I get paid for doing what I love and hopefully being useful to CEOs and executives. Working with CEOs, and coaching and mentoring their teams, has been a privilege and I have learned so much.

The list is a long one and my apologies if I have missed anyone out. I'll start with Dom Gaynor, who is CEO of TeamSport Indoor Go Karting. I watched Dom build a business from a few tracks in the south of England to become the number one indoor go karting business in the United Kingdom with 35 tracks today. Along the way, he has built an extraordinary team and created a culture built on values that are at the heart of what the business does and how it does it.

Jitesh Patel, or JP as he is known, has built an astonishing creative culture delivering office design and building to the biggest and best businesses in London. Like Dom, he is passionate about his culture and cares deeply about his people.

Jonathan Richards, CEO of Breathe, delivers the most beautiful HR software there is into the SME market across the United Kingdom. A testament to the business he has built is the many suitors there were before he finally sold to ELMO, an Australian provider of cloud-based software solutions, in 2020. Jonathan has no plans to move on, believing that his journey is not yet complete with Breathe.

Patrick O'Luanaigh, CEO of nDreams, is the most creative person I know. nDreams creates the most amazing games for VR headsets. I remember vividly when I first met Patrick over seven years ago, when VR wasn't a horse that everyone was backing, but Patrick held his nerve, built a high-performing team from across the industry and pushed on. His business is now the envy of many in his industry.

Rob May and his brother Dan, like the others, have become friends as well as clients. Passionate, driven and smart, ramsac continues to outperform its competition and deliver outstanding technology services.

Paul Martin, the CEO of Kelly's Storage, is a true entrepreneur, finding synergistic businesses that fit into the Kelly's family. His growth of the business has been a pleasure to watch. Nothing pleases Paul more than developing and enabling talent to grow in his business, and his leadership team is testament to his skills in this area.

There are many others who have made an impact on me as I have coached, consulted or supported them. They include Ben Wales, my co-host of the Gritty Leaders Club Podcast, Peter Joshua of MMRG, Ren Rufus of SI Capital, Ben Beaumont of 48.3, Andrew Harting of HWM Aston Martin, Jan Hansen of SAV Systems, Paul Greenhalgh of Skillwise, Andy Milner of DNAStream, David Batchelor and Dean Hobbs of Wills and Trusts, Doug Wood of Ideaworks, David Smith of SMC, Hugh Welch of SGS Kyocera, Jamie Joyce of Flexeserve, Neil Brodey of Norbar, Adrian Griffith of Oval Business Solutions, Rob Judd of Optima, Gary White of White Springs, Carole and Adam Blackford-Mills of MRS Digital, David Samuel of Eyesite Opticians, Alan Pearce of Harlow FasTech LLC, Simon Meaney of MTD Formwork, Ally Maughan of People Puzzles, Jen Raines of Your Right Hand, Jim Kirkwood of TTC, Wendy Bartlett of Bartlett Mitchell, Chris Gamm of The Springboard Charity, Paul Tomlinson of IEG4, David Ffoulkes-Jones of WDS Global, Morten Frimand of WSAudiology, Francesco Mereu of Toyota and John Niland of Mid Essex PCT.